THE
CHALLENGE
OF
CHRISTIAN
HEALING

THE
CHALLENGE
OF
CHRISTIAN
HEALING

STEPHEN PARSONS

First published in Great Britain 1986
SPCK
Holy Trinity Church
Marylebone Road
London NW1 4DU

British Library Cataloguing in Publication Data

Parsons, Stephen
    The challenge of Christian healing.
    1. Spiritual healing
    I. Title
    615.8'52   BT732.5

    ISBN 0-281-04223-3

            Typeset by Pioneer, Perthshire
            Printed in Great Britain by
            WBC Print Ltd, Bristol

Contents

This book is dedicated to Frances,
without whom it would never have been written

Preface

In recent years the books written on healing, Christian and otherwise, have numbered several dozen. Yet in spite of all these attempts to describe the nature of healing there are still widespread misunderstandings about what healing in a non-medical context is all about. There is also considerable confusion as to how Christian healing is in fact distinctive in a world where so many different methods of healing are on offer.

This book starts from the conviction that Christian healing has a distinct and unique role in the search for wholeness today. But unlike other books on the Christian ministry of healing, this study is consciously ecumenical, and assumes that we should not limit our apprehension of Christian healing to what our particular tradition finds acceptable. Just as the Church is larger than any one denomination, so Christian healing is greater than any single Christian expression of it.

It is as well to begin with some initial definitions of what we mean by 'healing' and 'Christian healing', so as to shed light on the rest of the book. By 'healing' we mean a capacity in an individual or a group to change for the good the course of a disease in another, whether physical or psychological in nature. This capacity to heal is variously regarded as a psychic or spiritual gift, and appears to involve the tapping of energies which so far are beyond the realm of conventional science to explain. Healing may also sometimes be understood as the calling forth of an individual's own self-healing powers by some as yet little-understood psychic communication between healer and patient.

'Christian healing' begins, not with speculations about the mechanics of what happens between healer and patient, but with the obedient response to Christ to heal the sick as well as proclaim the gospel. From the point of view of the one administering the healing and the one receiving it, the action is bound up with the belief and expectation that God's Kingdom can and does break through. Thus it has as its intention much more than physical or psychological healing on its own, but is open to an experience of forgiveness and a renewed relationship with God. Christians would claim that healing of the kind that operates outside the orbit of Christian belief at best falls short of 'Kingdom' healing, and at worst could involve dangers through an involvement with powers that may be far from divine in origin.

Christian healing and non-Christian healing are linked in so far as both appear to manifest power or energy in the healing act, but Christian and non-Christian healers would have different ideas about the source of this power. Non-Christian healers would say that the energy is there in the universe for all to tap, while Christians would regard the power as being that of God mediated through the Spirit to the believer. We should bear in mind that 'healers' operating outside a Christian framework are probably more numerous than those who use the Christian understanding. While this book is about the varieties of a specifically Christian experience of healing, it is written with some awareness of the other side of healing in this country. I have taken the view that non-Christian healers deserve to be understood far better than they have been up till now, and not simply condemned out of hand. The Church appears to know too little about its own healing ministry to be able to afford the indulgence of condemning others who operate outside its control or influence. Mainly through the medium of interviews, my aim has been to provide a renewed understanding of a Christian healing ministry. Perhaps this will also provide some means of evaluating the wider healing phenomenon which appears to be growing alongside the Church's own ministry.

A book of this kind could not have been written without the help of a large number of people. I must record my sincere and grateful thanks to all who spoke to me and freely allowed me to quote their thoughts and ideas. Among others that I talked with who helped to give perspective on the whole subject were David Bick, Leslie Giddens, Peter Dewey, Ludi How, John Tabor, George Thomas, Hugh Dickinson, James Turnbull, Bishop

Morris Maddocks, Bishop Graham Chadwick and members of the 1984 Conference for Laity at Swanwick from the Anglican Diocese of Liverpool.

Shelagh Jenkyns took on the long and difficult task of transcribing the tapes of my interviews. She did this with considerable skill and enthusiasm, saving me a great deal of labour and speeding up the production of this book by several weeks or even months.

I must record my thanks to Rob and Nona Bowring who made some suggestions and corrections in chapters 8 and 9 from the perspective of the scientist and philosopher respectively. Also I must thank Dr Richard Hardy, one of my parishioners, for detailed reading of the manuscript and for some suggestions for chapter 9. Finally I must mention my wife Frances, to whom the book is dedicated. It is out of her illness, patiently and bravely borne over several years, that it has come to be written. Her interest and commitment to all that this book stands for have made the final outcome very much more than just a journalistic investigation. Together we have seen the whole subject grow into a new way of life for us both. Her support during the long hours of writing (and the patience of our children Anna and Clare) have meant that the whole project has been completed in less time than I expected.

September 1985   Stephen Parsons

ONE

Introduction

The life of a parish priest rarely provides opportunities for a change of direction in his ministry. As the resource man for a parish or community he is expected to know what he is about, and this expertise is supposedly carried with him from college or from a previous job. The incessant demands being made on his time, and on whatever expertise he may have, leave him little time or energy for any fundamental questioning of his ministry or of the basic direction in which he is going in his leadership of the flock. This book is written by one parish priest belonging to the Church of England who has been forced very dramatically to look at what he is doing in his ministry. He has been made to look at large areas of his work with new eyes and discover new aspects of ministry which he had not thought existed. The book presented here starts from a position of intense questioning. The answers offered to those questions form the basic material of this work. Conclusions of a sort are found, but what is mainly offered is a presentation of a fair amount of material on one particular topic, namely Christian healing, with some thoughts of my own as to how we may interpret it and ponder its significance.

The event which forms the basis of all that follows took place in February 1983. The basic facts are as follows. On an evening in that month my wife, Frances, a chronic sufferer from rheumatoid arthritis, went to a meeting in Hereford organized by the supporters of an itinerant charismatic healer, Peter Scothern. At that meeting, at which I was not present, she received the laying on of hands. Over a period of a few weeks it became apparent that the disease had gone into reverse, and she was able to dispense with the drugs which had been causing her grievous side-effects. At the present moment, November 1984, as I write these words, her progress has been maintained, and she has moved with me into the discovery of a healing ministry for ourselves.

Every study and presentation of a Christian theme has a context. I feel it right to sketch the background of one particular priest, myself, to indicate something of where I start in my presuppositions. Throughout my life I have been aware of healing as being a concern of the Church, but I had never really been able to take it seriously, in that I had never encountered it at first hand.

My only personal experience of healing happened before I was able to be conscious of it. My mother tells me that as a small child of eighteen months I was once plagued by a chronic attack of mastoiditis for which the doctor was recommending an operation. Brother Edward of the Village Evangelists was staying with us at our Vicarage in Portsmouth, and he prayed with me. The pain went almost instantly, as assessed by the speed with which I fell asleep, and the operation was never performed. Later on in childhood, I was aware of Dorothy Kerin, the well-known pioneer of Christian healing, and I narrowly missed visiting her Centre at Burrswood while she was still alive. The choir at Canterbury Cathedral, of which I was a member, was sometimes called upon to sing a service in the chapel there, thanks to the enthusiasm of our headmaster, Clive Pare, for the cause. This was around 1957.

Another event which I now see with increased significance was the serious illness of one of the boys at the school. He suffered from tuberculous meningitis, and I learnt at the age of eleven the expression 'critically ill'. The whole school went into an almost continuous period of prayer lasting about a week. His recovery was commonly ascribed to that immense support of prayer by those who took part. It was not difficult at that young age to believe in a God who listened and acted accordingly. That experience left me with a sense of the power of intercessory prayer and the feeling that I should spend much more time doing it.

Public school and university days came and went without any addition to my wisdom in the matter of healing. I remember being challenged about my Christianity by a fellow undergraduate. My answer, which I remember, contained no mention of God's power to heal through our prayer. Somehow the God I was

2

learning to believe in had to be much more reasonable in the way he acted and behaved than the God of my childhood. A further incident took place while I was a student. Visiting Mount Athos in Greece, I was staying at one of the larger monasteries, and the group that was there at the same time included a hospital worker from Thessalonika. He organized a special service to pray for the sick at his hospital. We prayed in front of a large icon in flickering candle-light, and the scene moved me a great deal. The names of the sick were read out, and I pondered on this act of devotion, which seemed so right, even if my idea of God was not big enough to see how he could use it to help those we prayed for.

It would be difficult to describe exactly what I believed about God both as an undergraduate and a theological student. I suppose I was very caught up with the Anglo-Catholic ideals of priesthood, the pursuit of personal holiness, and the idea of God as beauty. Worship was the experience of being caught up in this transcending beauty. The spirituality I picked up was very much in the sacramental tradition. Devotion to Christ was centred in the devotion to the elements of the Eucharist. The reception of the elements was a high point in the week or, at theological college, of the day. Spirituality seemed to be something that affected only oneself, and I had no real idea that it was supposed to spill out to include other people, except in so far as one dutifully prayed for the needs of others and of the world. In this spirituality there was sometimes the feeling that part of what one offered to God was the sheer exhaustion of early mornings when one worshipped even though half asleep. God came to be the God of discipline, the God that could be satisfied by faithful but sometimes very arid spiritual exercises. As for God's being very interested in healing or physical wholeness, I saw little sign. My exposure to Eastern Orthodoxy in Greece had nevertheless taught me that God was interested in the body and in the emotions. My college sermon picked up this theme, and was an attack on the intellectual aridity, as I saw it, of much theological discourse. I used the image of a pair of binoculars, with each lens being one part of the personality, the intellect on the one hand and the emotions on the other. One had to use both lenses simultaneously to obtain a clear picture.

Life in a parish brought me into contact with a range of

experiences for which theological college had little prepared me. Two experiences particularly stand out from my early days as a curate. The first was constant exposure to sick and dying people. One could not chat aimlessly to a person in pain. There had to be something one could do. Gradually I learnt to pray with the sick, apart from the formal prayer set out for the Communion of the Sick. Formal prayer certainly played its part in helping the sick individual to come to terms with his or her pain, but what I found I needed was the ability to pray extempore. Once I had learnt to pray in this way I suddenly became aware of the fact that I was no longer alone in caring for the sick person. Both of us were caught up in a presence that was bigger than us both, and simultaneously we were united together closer than any conversation could achieve. This experience was particularly striking at times when I responded to an FDL (full danger list) call from the local hospital when the chaplain was off-duty. I always dreaded these calls, and would go with fear and trembling to the bedside. The amazing thing was that I invariably lost my fear and trembling once I got there, and was filled with a profound sense of peace which increased as I prayed with that sick person. Why I should feel united in prayer with a total stranger was always beyond me. I knew it happened, but never really thought about it at any length. In retrospect I can see that the experience of praying with sick people was as important to my growing spiritual awareness as the prayer in the Eucharist on which I had been nurtured. I was moving out of a reliance only on formal prayer to discovering also the power of the informal.

One sick person whose memory is very precious was a Mrs Vogt. I took her Communion every week, and my Vicar wisely did not interfere with this lavish attention to a single parishioner in a parish of twenty thousand souls. This old lady taught me a great deal about fortitude and faith in the presence of pain and decay, and this was of far more value than any help I was able to offer her. She was suffering from heart failure, with her limbs gradually filling with fluid. Hers was resurrection life in the midst of death. With her, prayer was in no way difficult, either formal or informal. I was very much expecting to be called to my first Christian death-bed with her, but she moved to a neighbouring town after I had been helping to care for her for about seven months.

The second influence on my spirituality was exposure to the Charismatic Movement from about the end of 1972. I was visiting in the parish, and came across a middle-aged woman who was in need of help and understanding after she had fallen out with her parish priest, the Vicar of a neighbouring parish. She and he had both received the 'Baptism in the Holy Spirit'. I then entered into a long and in many ways fruitful dialogue in which I experienced through her the agonies and the bliss of the charismatic experience. I was able to be positive about the whole thing because it fitted in many ways with my new insights about informal prayer, as well as with the Eastern Orthodox emphasis on the spirituality of the whole person. I recognized intuitively the link between the Orthodox 'Prayer of the Heart' and charismatic prayer. Both appeared to be using words, not for their rational content, but as a way of centring the attention on God. I cannot claim myself to have been initiated into the actual charismatic experience, but through this parishioner I came to a closer understanding of what was involved.

In the reading that I undertook at this time I soon discovered the healing dimension in the charismatic literature. I was struck by the passage in Dennis Bennett's *Nine O'Clock in the Morning* where he describes an involvement with healing as being 'part of the package'.

The charismatic experience and its possible implications for me personally as well as for my ministry were very much part of my preoccupation when I returned to Oxford to read for a research degree in 1974. I was disappointed not to find any charismatic group which I could join in my new-found freedom as a graduate student. I was not prepared at that time to search for charismatic prayer-groups among Evangelical Christian Union circles; I felt the gulf between me and them to be too vast. I did join a semi-silent prayer-group, and that helped me in discovering more about what was going on inside when external stimuli were taken away. The only charismatic incident that I experienced was attending, on one occasion, the meeting of a charismatic healing evangelist in the Clarendon Institute in Walton Street. His message was in many ways bizarre. He spoke about the Devil falling out of the upper air onto the earth, and that being the reason for all the troubles of the day. The strangeness of his message contrasted with the deep impression of his ministry of healing. People fell over after hands were laid on them, in the manner of many such meetings. I was at the time frankly puzzled, and yet at the same time moved. I felt a sense of power which brought me close to tears, and yet I was frankly irritated by the manner of his preaching. People I spoke to about this experience were of no help in interpreting it, and the incident passed to the back of my mind.

1976 saw me married to Frances and back in parish work as a curate in Kent. The charismatic interest in some ways declined, but, in one of the two villages I cared for, the whole informal side of prayer received expression in a small prayer/discussion-group that I started. This flourished, and needless to say I learnt a lot about what can be achieved in the atmosphere of prayer and sharing at a fairly deep level. Our first child, Anna, arrived soon after we arrived in Kent, so that my wife was unable to participate in what was a precious part not only of my ministry but also of my spirituality. My conversion to an 'Evangelical' informal spirituality thus went on. I continued to read books on the charismatic movement and healing, and was much impressed by Morton Kelsey's book, *Healing and Christianity*, which I read in 1978. This book is vital for an understanding of the reasons why the healing ministry declined in Christian history, and I summarize some of his arguments in chapter 9 below. My enthusiasm for the book then was such that although I had no experience of the healing ministry I felt moved to address the clergy chapter on the subject. My conclusion was that while we might not be called to a healing ministry ourselves, nevertheless we should take intercession for the sick far more seriously than we perhaps did.

After three years in Kent, during which time both our children were born, we moved to Herefordshire. Here I took up the incumbency of three villages outside Hereford. From the very beginning of our time in Hereford, Frances began to get ill with arthritis. After eighteen months her symptoms were severe enough to restrict her walking, and finally, in the summer of 1981, she was virtually bed-ridden and in serious and continual pain. We early on learned to interpret the statements of the doctors to mean that they could not hold out a great deal of hope for her, particularly after the most obvious drugs at their disposal failed to have any effect on the course of the disease. Healing through prayer and laying on of hands was one thing we explored, along with a whole host of alternative medical treatments. Some of these latter, particularly acupuncture, provided a degree of help, and the absence of side-effects in these treatments was a welcome feature of them. The particular ministry of healing that we discovered was a healing service locally, but after attending two or three times Frances came away discouraged. It was not just that she failed to receive any help, but that she detected in the services an air of impersonality about the whole proceeding. It was, as she put it, a 'sausage-machine'.

In the early part of 1982 I noticed that in the Shirehall in Hereford services of healing were advertised, conducted by one Peter Scothern. I made some enquiries about these to a Baptist minister of suitable charismatic pedigree, but he was not very encouraging. The set-up of the services was completely outside the organized churches of Hereford, and thus for him was beyond the pale. Chastened for even considering such a possibility, I put these services out of my mind. It was not until the beginning of 1983 that Peter Scothern's name came up from a completely different quarter. A friend had heard of someone who had been healed of cancer at these services, and urged Frances to go. In spite of all my experiences I felt uneasy. It was the organization of these meetings outside the sponsorship of any recognized Christian community in Hereford that worried me. Could this man really have something to offer that none of the main churches had? Also, while my experience of the charismatic movement was reasonably wide, Frances had never been exposed to anything like this: could her High-Church upbringing cope? But the situation at the time of her attending the first of Peter Scothern's meetings was far too worrying for these scruples and concerns to get the better of us. Ten days before the February meeting Frances's hospital doctor had rung with the news that the blood sedimentation rate which measured the activity of the disease was fast rising. This coincided with her coming off a particularly unpleasant drug. The Hereford doctor had rung a London doctor who had seen Frances some time before and who now insisted that she go back on to the same drug, although it caused her severe vomiting and malfunction of the kidneys. If this was all the medical profession had to offer at this stage, then we were not going to avoid an itinerant healer on scruples as mild as these.

Frances went to the Shirehall in Hereford that cold night in February with two friends, and I anxiously awaited her return. Her arrival back home was undramatic but she seemed very tearful. I asked what had happened, and her only answer was that she didn't know. She had fallen over when hands were laid on her, but apart from that, I could get no clear story. She then went to bed and started to cry and this went on all through the night. I assumed that once again she had suffered another disappointment, but in the morning she was much more peaceful and positive about what had happened. She felt sufficiently positive that something had happened to keep off the drugs that had caused her violent vomiting. The subsequent weeks confirmed the progress, and the next blood test showed a dramatic and sudden drop to a near normal figure. Her GP confessed himself amazed at this, particularly as she had abandoned the drug treatment that the London doctor had insisted on.

By the early summer it was generally known that my wife was improving, and that I could function at more or less full strength in the parish. It was in May that I encountered the Bishop in the cathedral, and he greeted me with the surprising news that he wanted me to be his Ecumenical Officer for the diocese. This appointment suggested that he had some confidence in my theological reliability, so I asked him if I could also keep him briefed on what I described as the Christian sub-culture in Hereford. I wanted to discover as much as I could about the various small charismatic and Evangelical groups in and around the city which seemed to have something to offer to the main-line churches. Somehow, having the Bishop's confidence made it easier to go into situations I might have felt hesitant about as a ordinary parish priest.

It is against this background, that I took on the project set out by SPCK to produce an account of the healing ministry in Britain today in a critical but sympathetic manner. The project fitted in with the new horizons that I was beginning to explore as Ecumenical Officer and as a priest wanting once and for all to understand the place and reality of healing in the Church and in its ministry. All the books that I had read were intended for readers with whom their authors had much in common. What about people who were not familiar with or did not accept the theological background of a particular author writing about healing? My vision was to sit at the feet of those who practised healing in a wide variety of contexts and let them speak and talk about what they did and understood about healing. I wanted to try to bridge the barriers of language and culture that I knew might arise, in very much the same way in which participants in ecumenical dialogue attempt to do so. In the event there were far fewer barriers to be crossed than I expected. The experience of being involved in a ministry of healing appeared to unite people across the barriers of denominations and theologies.

As soon as I had accepted the challenge to look at healing from this wide perspective, I realized how difficult this was going to be from a practical point of view. I possessed no contacts with the world of healing, and I wondered for a time whether anyone would in fact want to speak to me. My mind went first to contacting people involved with healing at the official level and in its organized form, such as the Guilds, the Homes of Healing and the various co-ordinating bodies. In this I found I could not get very far. For a whole variety of reasons, I found myself going beyond the organizational side of Christian healing, and moving out to discover the unaffiliated individuals and congregations who practise this ministry at a local level. In retrospect this was a right decision. I came to see that individuals are concerned for the pattern of healing which works for them. Their testimonies may have rough edges and imperfect theologies, and generally lack the rounded and tidy presentation of healing that belongs to groups or organizations representing large numbers of people. None of the people I interviewed are in fact linked with any of the main Christian healing organizations. But this does not lessen the value of their accounts: rather it bears witness to the vitality of this ministry, that it can grow and bear fruit with, initially at any rate, only the Spirit to guide.

We have then in this work some account of how Christian

healing is in fact practised from the point of view of individuals who have discovered this ministry more or less spontaneously. We should not be surprised that the insights and opinions of these individuals do not always conform with the norms of orthodox theology, but I hope they will be listened to with respect. Perhaps Christian healing will always challenge and disturb whatever orthodoxies we may have erected for ourselves, as it springs, after all, from the uncomfortable fact that God is active in the world today.

The early decision to go beyond the official structures of healing made my task of research much more difficult. The first couple of months were frustrating, as I had not realized how difficult it would be to find people willing to talk. The breakthrough came in February 1984, when I travelled to Exeter to meet Gibson Pattison, to whom I had been introduced by a Canon of Hereford Cathedral. In talking to Gibson I realized that his was a story which was unique, and well worth recording for the benefit of the wider Church. Gibson succeeded in convincing me that my plan to search out the unofficial face of Christian healing was eminently worthwhile. Here was a story of tremendous power and conviction. Listening to Gibson, one could not doubt the reality of healing, and I wished that he had been allowed to speak to the Archbishops' Commission in 1956, when there was such a strange reluctance to understand the nature of the healing gift.

As time went on the sense of doing something worthwhile continued with me. As I uncovered more and more people I asked the question, 'Has anyone heard this story before?' The answer was almost invariably 'No'. I began to see that what I was collecting was a unique compilation of testimonies of healing practice that might otherwise never have been expressed or heard. The healers I spoke to were without exception men and women of humility, who would not have told their story unless it had actually been requested of them. The other value of my travels which became apparent was that I was able to give a voice to individuals who, because of the fragmentation of the Christian Church into denominations and sects, would never normally be heard except by those among whom they move. Even healers belonging to the so-called 'extremes' I found to possess a reasonableness and accessibility to discussion that they are not commonly held to have. In no sense would I expect all readers of this book to agree with every sentiment expressed by those I have interviewed. But I hope that, having made theological and cultural adjustments in their position, they may recognize that the power of God to heal today is a reality, and that even those in profound theological disagreement will still find something to learn from each of the healers presented. The inclusion of so many different ideas is meant to stimulate readers into achieving for themselves an informed attitude towards the reality of Christian healing. I am not expecting them to agree with everything that is said about healing here!

Thus the presentation of the healing ministry of the Church in this study is not promoting particular styles of ministry to the exclusion of others. Indeed I hope that the study can serve a purpose by pointing, however dimly, to the full complexity of the pattern of Christian healing in this country today in its many forms and manifestations. Whatever theological study may be done on the topic of healing in the Church in the future, it cannot be done satisfactorily by those who see healing from denominational or sectarian biases. Christian healing is not only practised across every denomination, it is found in places outside what many of us would recognize as part of the Church. Healing not only presents problems to ecumenical theology, it also raises questions about what the visible limits of the Church are. But however these problems are to be solved, this book proceeds from the position that Christian healing is something far bigger than any one denomination or theological framework can contain. Any attempt to limit Christian healing in this way is bound to fail, just as trying to limit God to one particular theological language will always fail. Healing will always break out of the structures in which we may try to confine it, whether these are organizational or conceptual. It will be seen to be bigger than them all.

This book is humbly offered as the record of one man's search to discover the nature of Christian healing and its implications for the Church and the Church's ministry. It does not offer many answers, but it does provide material from which some answers may be extracted. As I have tried to demonstrate, we need to look at and understand the phenomenon of healing from many sides if

11

we are to grasp something of the nature of its reality. Healing, like many forms of truth, is to be compared to a diamond which glows with many facets. I hope that my readers may be led closer towards the reality of healing, so that they may experience it for themselves.

TWO

'Dedicated' Healers

The existence of 'natural' gifts of healing possessed by certain individuals is something that is recognized and accepted by people of every culture and religion, including our own. Indeed the word 'healer' tends to be associated in the ordinary person's mind with the so-called 'faith-healer'. But whereas in many other parts of the world faith healing and the healing message form the pivot of the activities of most of the prophetic independent Churches to which a large and increasing percentage of Christians belong, in Britain such healers will normally have little to do with Christianity or the Church. They may be religious in their attitude, but their religiosity will often owe more to Theosophy or Spiritualism than to Christianity. The reasons for this alienation from the Church of large numbers of people with healing gifts is beyond the scope of my study, but, in so far as it is true, I find it a cause for regret. A further cause for regret is the fact that many Christians look upon healing with suspicion precisely because so many healers belong to 'fringe' religious groups. Confusion abounds in this whole area, and few people are able to enter it with any degree of objectivity or understanding.

This chapter tells the story of three individuals who, in my estimation, appear to have healing gifts that exist 'naturally', or in other words, quite independently of the fact that each is profoundly Christian in outlook and belief. Their stories, and in particular the way in which they have integrated their natural gifts into a Christian framework, are the concern of this chapter. Each of them has 'dedicated' a natural gift or ability to the service of God so that it is used to his glory rather than their own. The accounts raise some interesting questions which have so far not been answered by the Church as a whole. How are such gifts to be evaluated? How are such individuals to be guided and supported in the exercise of such a gift, particularly when they are lay-people?

If the Church could find some answers to such questions, then perhaps it would not lose such individuals to the Spiritualist Church or one of any number of fringe spiritual groups. At the moment it could be claimed that such groups appear to have far more familiarity with 'natural' healing gifts than the Church does.

We begin the presentation of dedicated healers with the story of Gibson Pattison, a parish priest who works in a village outside Exeter. Gibson's story illustrates well the tension that can exist between the gifted individual and the structures of the institution which decide which individuals should exercise ministries in its name. His story would be a tidy one if his exercise of a healing ministry began with his ordination some twenty-five years ago, but in fact it presents the complete opposite. He exercised an effective healing ministry as a layman, but proceeded to lose it as soon as he became involved with the institutional structures of the Church. His original discovery of his healing gift in many ways parallels that of the healer, Bruce MacManaway. Both discovered their gift in the stress and strain of active service. MacManaway went on to develop his healing in a context away from the Church, while Gibson has remained within the Church, though not without incident.

I met Gibson in the village on the edge of Dartmoor where he is Rector. He talked of a ministry that had gone on over a period of forty years without any sensation or fuss. In describing the healing ministry he made it sound very ordinary and common-place, as though he was talking about the everyday work of every priest. And yet his story has many facets which make it far from ordinary and everyday.

The first healing that Gibson could recall took place in the last days of the war in Germany. He had a unit of a thousand men under his command, and among them was a Canadian corporal named Don. Don had a face covered with sores which had failed to respond to any of the treatments handed out by ten doctors. Gibson went on:

> We got to know each other fairly well. One day I had a feeling and said, 'Why don't we pray about it?' We did, and I went back to my

house — a German house we had taken over — and George my batman and I mixed up all the medicines we could find in the medicine cupboard in the bathroom. We took this strange mixture and gave it to Don, and I said, 'Put this on your sores and they will go in six weeks. Put it on as though the finger that puts it on is the finger of Our Lord, the finger of Christ.' He thought I was a bit dotty, but he did it, and the result was that everything vanished in three weeks. It was a strange business. But that gave me the idea that the real activity was prayer rather than the ointment.

Gibson recalled a further incident when a badly wounded Russian soldier was brought into his unit. While he was waiting for treatment, Gibson put his hands on the bleeding and it stopped immediately. But on his return to England after the war, his own Vicar refused to let him start exercising this laying on of hands. According to Gibson the Vicar told him, 'I've seen it done in Burma and it's all right there, but it's not right to go round laying hands on people freely.'

In spite of this unpromising start, the word somehow got around that Gibson could help the sick, and he recalled how a lady of the parish, a Mrs Wilder, came to see him. She asked him to come and pray with a man in his mid-forties who had had a bad stroke which had disabled him almost completely. This direct request emboldened him to go once again to the Vicar and tell him that he was going to respond to this request, asking him to come as well. At first the Vicar refused to come, and again tried to discourage him from going. But in the end four of them, Gibson, the Vicar, the curate and Mrs Wilder, met at the sick man's house for a service of prayer and laying on of hands. In Gibson's words:

> The man recovered instantly, that very moment, completely. He was able to move, walk about, talk, think and so on and so forth. And the miraculous thing to me was that there was a deaf-and-dumb boy of twenty-one in the room — I didn't know it at the time — who recovered his hearing and his speech. His hearing was complete but his speech took some time — some weeks. I realized that we were on the brink of a tremendous recurrence of New Testament times. This happened in 1949.

I asked Gibson how his Vicar had reacted. He mentioned that he was delighted, but that it was still extraordinarily difficult for him to fit it into the life of the Church because he had no established position in the structure. His ministry went on to develop in three directions. In the first place he started with Mrs Wilder a time of prayer in the church on Tuesday evenings, when he let it be known that the sick of the parish would be prayed for. People came to join him, and gradually the group grew, so that at its height it numbered some 250 people. At the same time he started praying with a small group of four, and this has been part of his practice on and off ever since. Thirdly, he found his individual ministry becoming more and more in demand, and he was called to pray with individuals at any time of day or night. Although by the mid-50s he had become a Lay Reader in his parish he felt that his ministry was not based in the parish, nor even in the Church of England, but was offered in the name of Christianity. He recalls how the doctors had looked on him with great suspicion, and he suspects that his approach may have been somewhat brash.

Gibson's healing ministry came to a temporary but abrupt end at the end of the 50s. The reason for this break is extraordinary, and it is important for us to ponder it in our attempt to understand the healing ministry in the Church. In brief, Gibson was, in his own words, 'hijacked into the Church of England as an ordained minister', and from the start of his training, as he put it, 'the healing ministry died on me.' Gibson's thoughts on why the healing ministry left him are extremely interesting. He felt suddenly restricted by being closely identified with a single church denomination, whereas before he had operated outside the formal church structures. Not only was he now formally linked with a single denomination but he was also given an authority which was institutionally defined. He had exchanged the authority he had, to gain an authority he had never wanted, 'the authority of a dog-collar'.

We are here entering a difficult area, the area of how the Church in its institutional aspect approaches healing. Clearly the Church has a role in protecting its members from excesses of doctrine and practice that may come from unauthorized practitioners of healing. But the task of protecting and authorizing can easily become a quenching of the Spirit of God. Gibson first began to exercise his ministry at a time when very few people in the Church of England appear to have had any understanding of the healing gift. The whole tenor of the report of the Archbishops' Commission of 1958 was towards a responsible and sober exercise of the healing ministry as part of the wider pastoral ministry of the clergy. It gave no guidance with regard to the evaluation or encouragement of distinctive gifts of healing in a lay person, apart from noting their existence. Even the participation by a lay person in a healing service required a bishop's permission. In short, Gibson's position in the fifties was completely outside what the institutional Church could cope with. It is small wonder that he experienced a dramatic change of role when he became ordained. Although an Anglican, he had had to free himself from the discipline of this church, and now he came into an institutionally-defined authority.

The existence of healing gifts in the Church outside the recognized centres of authority picks up a tension that has existed in religious institutions since the time of Amos and before. As a prophet, Amos challenged the *status quo* of the institutional religion of his time. Simultaneously he was himself a challenge to the organized prophetic religion of his time, for he was no 'prophet's son'. The Church cannot expect to confine God's activity within certain defined institutions. The 'charismatic' and prophetic voice has always to be listened to if a creative balance is to be observed. Gibson's implied challenge to the institutional Church needs to be evaluated with an open mind if we are not to be in danger of missing something that God could be saying to us today. We do not have to agree with everything he or any other prophetic voice might say, but, in his case, his healing ministry over forty years does give him a right to be heard, even if it challenges ways of thinking about that kind of ministry that we may formerly have adopted.

In spite of the loss of his healing ministry over twelve years, Gibson did not seem to have any regrets. His ministry as a priest had developed his healing gifts in new directions. He particularly valued the authority of the Church to announce forgiveness of sins, as this was an important aspect of much of his ministry with sick folk. His ministry now possessed greater depth, if perhaps lacking in the enthusiastic confidence that he had had as a layman. The sense of what was appropriate in a Church of England context had, he admitted, to some extent toned down his style. I asked then about his current ministry to individuals. He answered this by telling me about a woman he had ministered to three weeks before my interview with him:

Three weeks ago I got a phone call to go to a village in the middle of Dartmoor. I got it third hand from a deaconess who lives on the moor, who rang and said, 'So-and-so is seeking your help and won't take help from anyone else' (meaning clergy). So I found out who the Vicar was and I rang him. He said, 'Go ahead', when I asked him if I could go. Then I asked the Lord whether I should answer this call. He seemed to say yes. It's a feeling that this is right. There is no voice that says, 'Go forth, Gibson'. Sometimes there is something that says, 'No'. The intuition has gradually developed and I trust it much more now, though once I was very hesitant and suspicious. I think this comes from daily meditation. So I went over and found she was riddled with cancer. She had been in hospital and had several operations. She had had chemotherapy and had it in most parts of her body. She said, 'It's kind of you to come. I appreciate it so much. I once came to one of your Wholeness and Renewal services. The fact is I want to get back to that church, as I realize I'm wrong.' I said, 'Why? Explain it.' She said, 'What happened was, when we came into that church, you said that the door is closed upon all evil things, you are now at peace, you are now in the presence of the Lord, your healing has begun.' She said, 'I've never forgotten that. I've always wanted to get back into that security. I am now very weak and I want to make my peace.' So I said, 'What's been worrying you?' She said, 'How do you know?' And I said, 'It's all over your face.' She said, 'I have a daughter who is an epileptic and she has an illegitimate son through going to work in a college for the disabled; she came back pregnant. And I've worried about her.' And I said, 'Not only worried, but you have been really hurt by this, the fact that people realize that you have got an illegitimate grandson.' She said, 'Yes, that's quite true.' So I said, 'Have you forgiven your daughter?' 'Yes, but I haven't forgiven the man, though.' So I said, 'You must do so. And that is going to be difficult for you to do. You must do it. If you would like to make your confession sacramentally, I'd be glad to help.' Anyway, we prayed, and she poured out her heart to me, which is the first time she had ever done so to anyone; and I assured her of the forgiveness of Christ, which is something I *can* do better as a parson than as a layman. As I left her, her husband gave me four jolly good swedes as a present. I had a letter from her to say that she was still tired and she had had a remission from the cancer, the doctors were very pleased and she was up and about. When I was at the side of her bed I didn't feel she was going to get better. But my feeling is not infallible. When I pray I feel that I am a channel or pipe, and very often I am able to forget myself. I step out of the way and am a channel between God in Christ and the person. We link up with Christ and there is a kind of gathering in.

Gibson went on from this account of individual ministry to his activity within a small meditation/prayer-group. The group had been a feature of his healing ministry from the very beginning. The current group consisted of only three people. The concerns that were brought before them were not just for sick people, but for individuals with any kind of problem, such as unemployment. The method of prayer that they used was not what some people would understand as intercession. It was more a waiting on God, seeking to know his will in the particular situation. Once that will was known and revealed to all three in an identical way, they had complete confidence that God would act decisively for that individual. Sometimes the direction was given that they had to do or say something to enable the will of God to be fulfilled. He explained about it in the following way:

The three of us meet together; we have a light meal. We pray together and we ask God's will in any requests we are making before we make it. We may spend five or ten minutes or quarter of an hour seeking to get a direction. We each receive direction from God in different ways. One of us receives direction from God through a visual experience — he sees the person who is ill better, or who is looking for a job with a job — the other has a feeling about the direction. I have direction given to me through the mind, spiritually. When we come to an agreement in the direction we have been given, then there is the shout 'Amen'. We are sending a great force out of the room. Sometimes we are given instruction on what we should do. Perhaps we should go and see the person and tell them they are being prayed for. We are completely fearless in our outlook because we know that if we are agreed, we are right. We don't hesitate after, if for instance we get the direction that the person should cease taking his tablets. We will then go without hesitation to them, and involve the doctor, and say that after prayer we feel it would be wrong for this person to have these tablets, would you please check them. Doctors are gradually respecting us if we do it this way, rather than if we go and say, 'We know the answer'. Basically there is nothing we cannot do in the name of God. But I believe that the intention must be purified firstly by knowing that it is the will of God at that particular moment to do it. Every action of healing or ministry should be checked all the time. It may be God's will to do it today and not tomorrow.

Gibson did not put much stress on the fact that his group had effected the healing of many people. But he mentioned that he had never known anyone not to be healed when all three of them had received the same direction that it was to be so. The only actual incident that Gibson told was of a clergyman, whom I happened to know, who had recovered from a degenerating eye disease after he had been prayed for by Gibson's group. This was a story that I was later able to confirm from the individual concerned. The direction that the group received was often simply to give thanks that the problem or sickness that they had sought God's will on was being taken care of. The 'Amen' that they shouted out, when they had received an identical direction or awareness of God's will for an individual, was their contribution in a process whereby God's will became an actuality. Somehow the act of prayerful meditation and waiting on God could be used in a powerful way to help the individual. The stress on seeking the will of God first, before embarking on healing prayer, is very instructive. Perhaps most of us presume too much that we know God's will in detail for an individual before we pray for them. Gibson's comment on this, as well as his assurance that the will of God is knowable through the kind of profound meditation that he and his friends practise, is a valuable testimony in our attempt to understand the way that healing prayer works.

Gibson went on to tell me about the services of healing which took place in his parish and elsewhere by invitation. He believed that it was important to have lay participation in the formal laying on of hands at a service, no doubt to express the fact that healing is given to the whole Church. Normally there will be three individuals offering this ministry at the altar rail. Those who are seeking healing or help for themselves or another come up two at a time at opposite ends of the rail, so as to preserve total confidentiality and make it an individual ministry. Gibson told me that he acts as the third minister, joining one of the others when he feels it necessary. The individual is encouraged to express the prayer that is requested, and as Gibson put it, 'It has got to be positive, and it has got to be to our Lord with the eyes on him and not on us.' When the individual comes up on behalf of another person, Gibson told me, 'I thank God that they are there as an intermediary or intercessor, and we together in Christ make this request for John that he may be renewed, may be strengthened, given confidence in his exams or whatever.' He added that anointing with oil might sometimes be used as well as laying on of hands. This might be either at their request or when the minister feels it helpful. He went on:

> And we give thanks at the end of every ministration that God has taken the disease into his heart, whatever it is. We don't normally mention the disease by name and we ask people not to mention it when they come up. We ask them to ask for strength and for healing. But the tendency for unthinking people is to say, 'Please God will you help my rheumatism', and that always makes it worse because they are not being positive.

Gibson told me about his approach to preaching at services of healing. He felt that only a limited amount could be got over in the sermon. He tended to concentrate on the practical points of the service and the fact that the intention was not only to be healed but also to grow in Christ. He also tried to get over to them that through their suffering they might be able to grow. He would stress the fact that at the altar rail there was no overhearing of confidences, and that they could speak freely with their requests.

The services themselves, Gibson said, were seldom marked by any outward emotion. Only one young man had ever fallen over after having hands laid on him, and he found out afterwards that this man had not eaten all day. Occasionally people broke down and cried. But for himself Gibson spoke of occasionally having warmth in his hands or a certain trembling and vibration. Sometimes the people to whom he ministered noticed warmth when he was not aware of it himself, and at other times it was true the other way round. There was no regular pattern to the mood and atmosphere of these services, except that he felt a deep sense of gratitude every time, which he felt permeated the whole event. In every situation he had a sense that a prayer offered for another person had an effect. The prayers that he used in his public ministry were never according to a fixed pattern, but he prayed according to what he felt he had been given. People many times confirmed afterwards that he had said just what was right. For this he took no credit, it was all part of ministry in and through the power of the Holy Spirit.

I questioned Gibson more closely on his understanding of healing and how it fitted into his understanding of God. He admitted that his journey into Christianity had been anything but orthodox. His questioning had started at school:

When I was at school, I became disillusioned with the Church of England — that's not uncommon. I felt they were so far lacking the spiritual power of Jesus and the early Church that they were falling into an abyss. So I rejected and got fed up with all the paraphernalia of Anglo-Catholic worship, red slippers etc. I enjoyed it — I enjoyed the theatre of it — but I fould it a bore eventually because it didn't mean much to me. I sought the permission of the chaplain to have my own services rather than attend chapel. I think he was pretty wide-minded, because he allowed me to. I'd never have done it if I'd been a master. Then I left the school and got involved in the army, and I started to travel metaphorically through the Indian and Eastern religions and philosophies. I spent three or four years trying to understand Buddhism, a bit of Zen and some Hindu philosophy. The result of this was that I was convinced that there was one God, that there were a myriad different ways of approaching him for mankind, but through Christ there was a cosmic connection of man with God, an inevitable link — that the body of God was sent down so that we could be redeemed and reconciled. All the other religions, unfortunately for them, do not yet know this. But with this background my views became much wider, and yet I was narrower in the sense that I had felt compelled to come back to Christianity. It was the only thing that suited my temperament and my being. Churchianity I began to despise. People need to learn first of all to overcome their prejudices, and this can best be done by giving them a wider view of God — of his being almost pantheistic, that he is everywhere and that nothing can exist without him. We move and live and have our being in him. He is in us — I think that this is the first basic teaching. God is a fact for Eastern religions, and he is outside time and space. In order to contact him properly we must be prepared to move into that dimension. Jesus when he ascended did not go upwards; he moved into another dimension and he is still there. God is everywhere and anywhere. There is no such place as a God-forsaken place and no such person as a God-forsaken person. These kinds of ideas are essential before we know how to pray — that's wrong — before we can pray with that absolute security that the prayer is heard and real. People who want to heal, to put their hands on people to heal through love, must have the basic knowledge of the philosophy of God as I have described it. A lot of people in the Church, not only lay, who ask me to direct them how they can be used in the healing ministry are not prepared to go outside the Church because they are so tied up with the correct way of doing things. Someone asked me the night before last why I used my thumb when I anointed them. I'd never thought about it but I have done it automatically. Now I shall have to think whether it's the right way or not.

Gibson was evidently expressing some impatience with a churchy way of doing the ministry of healing which emphasized a correct way of doing things at the expense of a basic understanding of God and a relationship with him. His 'broad' doctrine of the nature of God, which borrowed some of its language from the other great religions, derived not so much from his ideas or even his study, but more from his practice of meditation for forty-five minutes every day. He had spent three weeks in 1953 with an Indian fakir and a Buddhist monk learning how to meditate, and clearly this activity was important both to his spirituality and to his ministry of healing. It enabled him to enter the 'other dimension' and be in tune with the 'Cosmic One'. Although his healing ministry was founded on a natural psychic gift, Gibson felt that the gift was developed and sustained by meditation and prayer. The psychic natural dimension of healing went side by side with the disciplined spirituality necessary to exercise the gift.

The language of the 'Cosmic One', and the apparent pantheism of his way of talking about God did not prevent Gibson from having a deeply-held doctrine of Christ. Christ was described as 'the individualization, the personalization of God'. 'This', he told me, 'is directed into the figure of Christ, into the personality of himself as a man.' He went on:

To me Christ is a constant companion — he is the same as the Cosmic

One but he is another expression of the Cosmic One. Here we are using language of experience rather than theology. I think the individualization of the One is represented by the figure of Jesus Christ. In other words Jesus Christ helps us to realize our personality in the midst of all the impersonality of the One. I can talk to Christ, whereas I don't talk to God — I'm part of him. This sounds dotty. If I am ministering in church in the name of Christ I'm aware that the power of the Cosmos, the power of God is being directed through the vision of this one perfect catalyst, which is Christ.

At this point I added the comment that the catalyst of Christ was perfect not only because he expressed the One, but also he had totally involved himself in the world through incarnation and suffering. He went on to say how important the figure of Christ was when going into places of evil: 'Christ is with me and I try to inculcate this into people who are scared of or frightened of things. I always advise people who come for healing to keep away from anything they don't understand except trust in Christ.'

It was clear to me that Gibson was speaking out of a profound depth of experience, rather than telling me the words he thought I wanted to hear. The very difficulty of expressing his ideas clearly was in itself a testimony to his deep insights and profound spirituality, which are the context of his healing ministry. Belief was not something inherited by being a member of a particular community. It was something that emerged out of the depths of this experience.

Many Christians would find exploration of the spiritualities of other religions quite difficult to countenance, and thus the story of Gibson is not one with which they can easily identify. But the final destination which Gibson has reached might suggest that the end justifies the means. The story of Gordon, a priest of the Church of England involved in healing and counselling, is one that introduces some elements which are even more unusual. Gordon in brief discovered — or perhaps he would say rediscovered — psychic gifts of healing much later in life than Gibson, but he too found these gifts developing when studying in areas both within and beyond the boundaries of traditional Christianity. He has gone on to maintain a relationship with and understanding of the world of what might loosely be called 'alternative spirituality'. The rest of us should be grateful for his work in an area where few are brave enough to become involved. In all these researches he would claim that his faith in Jesus Christ was his anchor-hold.

Like most things in Gordon's life, his career as a priest fails to conform to a conventional pattern. Ordained at forty-two in the Diocese of Hereford he spent some nine-and-a-half years as a country priest before leaving the full-time ministry in order to train as a professional counsellor. Although past retirement age, his work now includes counselling men who have a history of violence towards their wives, and he also acts as a spiritual director for many people, both clerical and lay. His reluctance to remain in the full-time parochial ministry came as the result of being presented with more and more parishes to care for until he ended up with eight churches and seven parishes. It was not the pressure of work that concerned him — rather the increasing distancing effect from his parishioners that responsibility for so many parishes forced on him. He also became increasingly uneasy at being forced to play a particular role as Vicar, and in the process being in danger of losing his real identity. As he put it:

> You go into a country parish and people have certain expectations. Before you know where you are, they've actually placed you in a role, and the easiest way to play it is to role-play, especially if everyone is saying, 'Our Vicar is a lovely man.' I then thought, 'Somewhere in all this confusion I'm beginning to forget who I am, and I am not being true to myself.' So I just said to Mark Hodson (who was Bishop then), 'I'm sorry, I'm resigning. I need time to think things out.' He was not pleased, and he said, 'Oh, I've given you too much to do.' And I said, 'That may be true, but if I can't go into any farmhouse or any cottage in my parishes and know the children by name and know for example that Jean aged sixteen is pregnant and daren't tell her mother and that she'll come and talk to me about it — unless I have achieved that sort of relationship I don't think I'm exercising the cure of souls.' He said something to the effect, 'Oh, you can't think in these terms nowadays.' So I said, 'Well, when I was instituted I was told to take the cure of souls in this parish and this is the area I feel I've got to work in.'

Gordon resigned from the full-time ministry in 1969 and went off to work with Dr Frank Lake, the Christian doctor and psychiatrist, at the Clinical Theology Association in Nottingham.

The work he did in training for counselling involved him in some fairly soul-searching and traumatic experiences of his own. For some six months he entered a 'dark night of the soul' experience and, after pulling through this, he found a new stage in his life developing. Psychic gifts which had been with him since childhood were recognized by some of the people around him, and because of this he could learn to understand people better and explore them further. He described these gifts as nothing more than the reawakening of a kind of animal radar-system. It had been his observation that such gifts often belonged to those who had experienced a lonely and isolated childhood, or like him had lost their mother in early childhood. When seeking ordination he had spoken to his bishop about his 'strange ability to read people's minds, know what they were thinking and what they were going to do. I said that while it was useful in business, it should be put to a more altruistic use, to the service of God through his Church. The Bishop assured me he knew what I was talking about.'

It was now several years later, after leaving the parochial ministry, that Gordon was told that he had the gifts of a healer, that he possessed a healer's hands. It was recommended that he study with one Father Andrew Glasewski, a Polish Roman Catholic priest, who was chaplain to Polish displaced persons in the West of England and who lived near Newton Abbott. Father Andrew was expert in many aspects of the psychic, and was deeply immersed in the Jewish Caballah. The Caballah is a text-book of a rather esoteric mysticism, and some recognize in it a fairly comprehensive map of the human sub-conscious. Gordon learnt a great deal from Father Andrew's extensive knowledge of many spiritual traditions, and so for a period he was able to combine counselling training with, coincidentally, the sharpening of his natural psychic faculties. Also he was developing a growing discernment, and later he began to practise healing in the widest sense of the term. He found himself at this time counselling young people who had become hopelessly disoriented by dabbling in fringe spiritualities, combined sometimes with the use of drugs.

One particular experience that Gordon had when working with Father Andrew was described. They had been standing on some cliffs in Cornwall, and Father Andrew had said to him, 'I want to teach you to listen to the music of the natural order. I don't have to tell you that everything is a variation on an atomic theme which is vibration, and at a certain level of consciousness it can be interpreted as music.' Gordon went on:

> He was one of those extraordinary people who with no word spoken knew where you were in meditation. He possessed faculties often associated with Eastern gurus although he was a Catholic priest. He said, 'Don't just listen to the double basses of the cliffs or the first violins of the grass, fit the whole thing together — listen to the whole thing. When you listen to an orchestra you let the whole thing play through you.' I then had this fairly classic mystical experience where I was the cliffs, I was the sea and I was, I suppose it sounds presumptuous to say it, just for a fleeting second at one with the One that is All in all. I wasn't over against anything — I was everything. And it seemed to change my whole outlook. Every now and then I think, 'I'd like to get back to that', but a voice says, 'I think once is enough, you know now.' The resulting benefit seems to have been a deep underlying sense of security.

The approach to healing that Gordon developed during his time with Father Andrew was what he called a listening attentive ministry, a kind of total attuning to the person in front of him. Father Andrew had stressed the importance of the words of the *Shema Israel*, 'Hear, O Israel'. He had said, 'It's listening with every fibre of your being, and a big first question raised by disease is "What is it saying?"' Gordon gave me one example of how his sharpened psychic awareness had helped him to get to the root of a problem in the case of a fifty-year-old man:

> I suddenly saw his mother standing by the mantelpiece and realized that the mother-son relationship was so unhealthily bonded that this fifty-year-old man hadn't got away from his mother yet, he hadn't broken the emotional umbilical cord although Mother had died some time ago. This was mainly his disturbance.

But the psychic awareness and discernment that Gordon possessed also proved sometimes to be a great burden, and he found himself using it less and less as he developed a style of spirituality and prayer that was less dependent on this kind of experience. He still found himself able to use the attentive listening taught to him by Father Andrew, but he knew that he had to be firmly rooted in

Christian prayer before he could seek truly to help other people. For him the point of prayer and meditation was to find . . .

> . . . the still point in the centre of the whirlpool of psychological, sexual and mental drives. You can't see this as long as you are moving — you can't see the movement unless you stand still. From then on my healing and my meditation started from a prayer basis and a basis of inner stillness. That stillness will evoke stillness in another person. You want a patient to be able to say, 'Oh Gordon, I don't know what it is, but when I come and sit with you I seem to get my initiative back and I know I can deal with my problem.'

Gordon went on to tell me about one particular healing incident which had stuck in his memory, and which for me summed up his approach to the practice of healing. A woman came to him for healing with a kidney problem, which had been labelled terminal. The important thing for Gordon was the establishment of an aura of peace, love and understanding in the situation. As he put it:

> We arrived at a situation where we were not consciously working as priest/parishioner — not working as the healer and the patient. We were just two human beings listening to a situation and watching it. You have got to reach a point of the 'two or three gathered together in my Name', i.e. in complete trust, complete love and complete understanding, and then the 'I AM is in the midst'. All the Vicar-pantomime and all the healer-pantomime just disappears — there are just two human beings listening to a situation and watching it. There is a level of silence that is true communion.

I pressed Gordon to fill out this account to help me understand the whole process. He explained how he had gently led the woman to a new self-understanding through showing her, for example, how our strong dislikes of people are often because they mirror some of the things that are wrong with ourselves. After this Gordon had 'listened' with his psychic sensitivity. At one level he picked up the physical things that were wrong, and he also knew things at a deeper level:

> I was beginning to know all the things she had tried to tell me in words and a tremendous closeness came — really a kind of communion. And then I went in front of her and we looked into each other's eyes. It was, I believe, Christ in me looking at the Christ in her and there was no threat. We actually could look deep into each other's

eyes in complete trust. I didn't want to put my hands on her head because I thought that there was something paternal about that and that it was at that moment an inappropriate symbol. Afterwards I said, 'Go and lie on your bed — have a sleep for an hour. I believe something beautiful has happened. Don't go and do things directly — just go and lie down.' She said, 'I shan't sleep. I can't sleep for long at night and I can't sleep in the daytime.' So I left her and went to talk to her Vicar till 5.30, when her husband returned. She met me at the door at 5.30 and she was absolutely glowing with a tremendous look of wonder and joy. She said, 'I slept. It's years since I slept like that.' I met her Vicar about a fortnight later and I said, 'I haven't heard anything from Judy.' He said, 'I don't know what you've done to her but she has done nothing but sleep. And another thing, she's been to her doctor and he's cut down her drug dose.'

Gordon then completed the account by describing to me the kind of prayer that he would offer in a case like Judy's:

It's usually quite a simple prayer. 'Lord of all being, you have once more enabled me to feel at one with the totality, once more you have placed me in a place of security, once more I can touch the infinite security and timeless peace, enable me to share this with the other human being so that in these moments of peace, strength and security, the psyche and the body may be able to do what they are intended to do.' I knew that if that peace could sink into her long enough the deterioration process might be thrown into reverse and the dear old body would begin to do what God created it to do. I then sink into complete silence. In my language, if you can touch that innermost peace for a moment or two, that is when somehow or other the whole being recaptures and gets caught up in the divine initiative and everything begins to recover harmony. The discord is thrown into reverse. The result sometimes of course is to enable them to die without fear and in faith, which is an aspect of healing. At the end of one year she was completely recovered.

The story that Gordon told had a sequel. Three years later the woman rang up to tell Gordon of a little girl of three who was suffering from terrible eczema:

'She's rubbing her face on the dry grass and the ground until it bleeds. I can't stand it any longer, will you come and give her healing?' I told her, 'I can't come for three days, but think back into that silence, into your own experience of healing, try and piece it together again and try and draw that little girl in your imagination into that stillness. I'll come on Wednesday.' This was Monday. I arrived as promised. She met me at the gate with a sheepish smile and said, 'I suppose I ought to have told you not to come — come and have a look.' In forty-eight hours the scales had fallen off that child, her eczema had vanished. So I said, 'Well, there you are, join the club. You can share what you have received.'

The whole question of group healing then came up. Gordon himself was involved with various meditation-groups which from time to time practised healing meditation. Gordon was aware of a psychic healing power which could be generated in a group, which has little to do with real spiritual healing. He told me about the time when an old lady who was a member of the group had fallen backwards out of a bus and hurt her neck. The group had put forward her name and the thoughts of the group were directed towards her. One of the group, a chiropractor, declared that the lady was now all right because he had somehow, through psychic sensitivity, picked up the fact that the displaced bone in her neck had righted itself. Twenty minutes later the lady rang to thank the group very much for what it had done. She was out of pain:

> We thought about this and we analysed it and said, 'That isn't spiritual healing, it's psychic healing.' That was the power of the group, and I subsequently went on to realize that it was possible to do the most extraordinary things through so-called psychic healing, but unless you have dealt with the spiritual and psychological dis-ease, i.e. the psychosomatic causes, and healed the whole person, you can very often put things right physically and then often, about three months later, the person would be all to pieces again. Many doctors assure me that more often than not disease or pain is a signal of underlying dis-ease at a psychological and spiritual level. Jesus made this abundantly clear, e.g. 'Whether it is easier, to say, Thy sins be forgiven thee; or to say, Take up thy bed and walk'.

Gordon was repeating what Christian healers said to me time and time again. Every disease operated at more than one level. It was possible to remove the symptoms of the illness using conventional or non-conventional means, but unless the underlying causes were dealt with, little would be achieved in the long term. If the cause of the illness was basically spiritual, then spiritual means were needed to tackle it. Even when the root of a disease lay in childhood trauma it was often possible to speed up or even bypass the process of psychotherapy by spiritual means. An individual might find miraculous release from these traumas in the presence of someone who knew the meaning of 'shalom', the rootedness in the One who is at the centre of all that exists.

I asked Gordon the question that may be in the mind of many of my readers: What is the place of Christ in this whole system and understanding of healing? His answer was not what I had expected. His answer began within two quotations from the Bible:

> 'It is expedient for you that I go away, for if I do not go away the Holy Spirit, the Comforter, will not come to you. And if I go away, I will send him to you.' 'I am the door.' In what we term 'the Grace of Our Lord Jesus Christ', I often wonder if there is not a moment of psychic communication with the man Jesus which is like passing through a door, you mustn't hang on to it. He touches you and says, 'Go on, you've got it now, do it. Don't hang on to me like a Daddy − I'm teaching you how to be a whole human being.' When Jesus says at the end of St Matthew's Gospel, 'All power in heaven and earth has been given to me', and a bit later, 'I am with you always', it isn't 'I, Jesus', it's 'the I AM' − 'all that I have represented to you is available to you − all power in heaven and on earth is given unto you − now − wake up and find out what that means.' So I tend to avoid what you might call Jesuology and say 'Yes, you are the door.' For me, Jesus is 'the key to the Divine Harmony'.

Readers may find that this is not worded in a way that we would expect of conventional Christian theology. But once again we must insist that due recognition be given to the fact that Gordon is struggling to make sense of the reality of the power of God as he experiences it. If we are able to recognize in his experience an authentic Christian ministry, then we must give him considerable freedom in the way he chooses to express this experience. Hitherto the Church has given scant recognition to the psychic gifts of which Gordon speaks, and still less help in actually talking about them.

Gordon finished by telling me something more about those who had inspired and helped him in developing his healing ministry. He mentioned Mother Mary Clare of Fairacres Convent in Oxford. Like him she possessed psychic gifts, and had learnt to dedicate them to the service of Christ and humanity with the help of Fr Gilbert Shaw, the well-known Anglican spiritual director of the early post-war years.

He left me with one final comment about priesthood: 'Priesthood is the sharing of "wholeness", body, soul and spirit, and is in itself none other than a ministry of healing as exemplified in Jesus Christ.'

The final person I wish to present in this chapter is a lay-person whom I shall call Helen. Helen is a person who possesses a healing gift, which for many years she accepted without any real understanding or questioning. It appears to be true that women possess psychic gifts more commonly than men. The tragic accounts of trials of witches in the seventeenth century perhaps bear this out. The victims were often those unfortunates who, for no fault of their own, possessed psychic abilities of various kinds. While psychic abilities can be, and were, used for evil and selfish ends, equally they can be used for the help and service of God and of other people. Helen may perhaps be seen as typical of a possibly large group of women who possess gifts of a psychic kind, but who have been unwilling or unable to share discussion of them with other people. When I first met Helen, she told me that she had only shared the fact that she possessed a healing gift with her Vicar the previous autumn. She had never before felt able to talk about it to a clergyman; indeed its relevance to her practice of the Christian faith had only become clear to her over the previous few years. It had not only become relevant to her understanding of her faith, but was a key part of her understanding of the content of Christianity and her own vocation within it.

Helen's story is important for two reasons. First she has developed a natural or psychic healing ministry free from help or encouragement from others, whether from a Christian, Spiritualist or Theosophical viewpoint. Her healing ministry had not become locked into a particular theological perspective or tradition. There was in her account an innocence and simplicity. The second important aspect of her witness was the way that her healing gift had allowed her to penetrate the heart of the meaning of the gospel and the place of healing in it. Her involvement with healing also brought her into a direct and immediate encounter with the healing Christ. In other words Helen expresses in words of experience the profound truth that the gospel of Christ is about salvation: the healing and restoration of body, mind and spirit.

Helen's story begins in a fairly typical way. As a child in Liverpool in the years after the last war she went through a Baptist Sunday School, later knowing the same doubts and questions that she thought typical of teenagers. A particular crisis blew up when she realized that the adults who had upheld strict moral standards, and had been to her as gods on pedestals, nevertheless had feet of clay. From her early years, and more especially after she was married, she discovered that she had the capacity to calm people who came to pour out their troubles to her:

> I would really only listen. I couldn't help really in any way apart from listening, but they would always come to me whatever the situation and go away again happier. They would say, 'Well, things worked out as you said they would.' Whether it was psychological or not, I just knew that things would be OK.

The gift of creating a sense of calm in other people might not seem very remarkable, and even the ability to know the outcome of other people's problems only achieves its significance in the light of what these gifts turned into. Helen has no doubt that the gifts she possessed at the time when she had no particular religious faith were the prelude to her ability to achieve actual physical healing in those who came to see her. From being able to empathize with another at a deep level there came the impulse sometimes to lay hands on the person before her. But this transition was linked up with a series of events which led her in the end to two religious experiences of a fairly dramatic kind. Before this she had for four or five years begun to read her Bible and pray, and 'Slowly but surely I began to get a strong faith. I was open to Jesus and he really came into my life.' This first experience came at around the same time as her daughter was confirmed, and she was confirmed a year later. Then, as she put it, 'I began to use the gift in a more confident way.' But in spite of her new relationship with Christ and the Church she did not feel

33

able to share this with her Vicar. It was still very personal to her, and she had an idea that people might feel her strange if they knew about it. She went on to mention that she had needed a lot of time to develop in maturity and understanding, to be able to cope with the gift. At the time of her confirmation in 1979 she had reached forty years of age.

The experience which Helen next recounted was one that I found deeply moving. It possessed the character of being utterly self-authenticating, as well as being put in language which was totally fresh and uncluttered with religious jargon:

> I work for an estate agent in Liverpool and I have my own small office which I find very comfortable. In an office of this kind, there are times when we are madly busy and everything has to be done by yesterday, and other times when things are fairly slack. During these slack times I have the opportunity to reflect and read my Bible. One day I was reading the passage where it said 'Jesus wept'. It just hit me — it had such an impact. Jesus was crying. He had this marvellous news, what a good life people could have, how they could enjoy the world and be themselves, how people could be whole, be healthy. In a flash I just knew this and I cried. I really cried because I knew why Jesus was crying. That was the moment when I knew he was my friend. I started to understand and see people so much more through his eyes. It may sound strange but I could see how easy it was for them to change their lives. I began to realize that what was in my head, what I knew about healing, was God's great gift to me.

Helen in a flash was caught up in an identification with Christ, so that she was able to grasp the essence of what he came to bring and the way in which she was part of that process of bringing healing and wholeness to the world. The content of the message had become so clear to her that she confessed herself angry and frustrated at the way people chose to distance themselves from it. This insight helped Helen to understand the Bible with new clarity, and she recognized with a certain trepidation the enormous power God puts at the disposal of Christians who really believe. She told me, 'We shouldn't limit God's power. If we really believe, we can do and be whatever we want to be.'

Helen spoke about her experiences of healing in fairly general terms, and found it quite difficult to remember individual episodes. She spoke of only two incidents. The first was her visit to a woman who had both emotional and physical problems, the first connected with her marriage:

> After church one Sunday morning I really felt I wanted to go and see her, and I did. She told me, 'I'm so glad you've come, I was hoping that you would.' I sat with her, rubbed her back, and prayed with her. She did improve, but she is a person of a very nervous disposition, and there must have been some sort of block because the improvement got so far and no further.

The second occasion was when another woman came to visit her with a problem in her leg. She in fact asked Helen to put her hand on her and the pain left never to return. In talking about these events Helen described the feeling as though she were a channel. She told me later in the conversation that in offering healing she felt herself to be part of a divinely creative movement towards individuals. She was in some way mediating God's power and wholeness. Part of our conversation touched on the way in which these experiences were shared by her daughter of twenty-one. Helen recognized in her daughter the beginning of the same sensitivity and spiritual make-up as in herself. Spiritual stillness was what she found natural, and one would describe them both as natural contemplatives. Her daughter, she realized, had still some considerable way to go in recognizing the spiritual dimension of the gifts that they both enjoyed.

Helen recognized that she was in many ways at the beginning of her healing ministry, and she was in a quiet way starting to press that it should be recognized in her parish. She had, the week before my interview, addressed the PCC on the subject of the conference on healing where we had met. Helen's story, though only now really beginning, is worthy of our attention because it shows in a moving way how one individual was able to grow in wisdom and stature in and through a natural gift of healing. Without the quiet seeking for God which had gone on more or less all her life, one wonders where her gifts might have led her. Even now she is in much need of support and the right kind of encouragement that her gift be valued and used both within and beyond her congregation. We hope and pray that she will indeed find that support.

THREE

Charismatic Healing in the Parish

When I first made plans for this book, I had in mind a chapter on a parish which had become charismatic and had thus taken into its system a healing ministry. A parish of this kind was recommended to me in Yorkshire, but I felt that distance would make it impossible for me to do more than pay a quick visit. Also I was finding by this stage in my research that the testimony of individuals had a particular value which it was not possible to convey when one described the activity of whole groups of people. After correspondence with a contact in Gloucestershire I came to hear of a healing ministry formerly centred on the Roman Catholic parish of Chipping Campden. But what I discovered to be the situation was a ministry which, though based in the parish and reaching out beyond it, had not been acceptable to more than a few within the congregation itself. Both the charismatic dimension and the healing ministry of the parish were confined to a small prayer-group, and this group very soon became ecumenical, with Methodists and Anglicans joining in. I have nevertheless included the story of Chipping Campden because it is a story that begins within an ordinary parish, involving both priest and lay-people. In fact the story centres on two particular lay-people, a couple, Joan and Les Smith, who received Baptism in the Holy Spirit and, having obtained the help and encouragement of their parish priest, Father Peter Jones, went on to exercise a healing ministry in the whole area. The story is an important one because it tells how such a ministry was given to ordinary lay-people in a fairly conventional parochial setting. The story might have had a less happy ending had they not succeeded in taking their parish priest with them in their healing adventure.

Joan Smith no longer lives in the Chipping Campden area, and so this is a record of a ministry that to a considerable extent ended with the death of her husband some two years ago. Les died of cancer, and many will remember seeing him on the television programme 'Encounter' during his last days. He was interviewed by David MacInnes on his hopes and expectations as a Christian faced with death. When I visited Joan in the early autumn of 1984 I was privileged also to meet Father Peter Jones who had shared in their ministry. I first asked Joan about the origin of the ministry and the experience of Baptism in the Holy Spirit that had preceded it. She told me first of all about what led up to this experience:

> It was at a time when everything was going wrong in my life — I had a mother dying of a rather horrific cancer of the throat. She was a lovely lady and I was quite angry with God, and then I began to wonder if he was even there. And several things in the family happened which were rather traumatic. I was left with realizing that I had nothing to fall back on. Perhaps my religion had been doing all the right things but hadn't any depth to it. There was a kind of dryness of going through old routines — you can say the Lord's Prayer without even thinking a word of it. There was also this terrible longing, a hunger within me for something. It was about that time that I started reading, and I had one or two little flutters from God, so he was saying, 'I'm still around.' I suddenly realized that it's no good talking about God, I had to get into some sort of relationship with him. And that meant a discipline. And that is how it built up, the reading and the need for a spiritual discipline. When the girls had gone off to school — they were quite young then — I settled down. First of all it was for twenty minutes, and it grew.

Joan then went through a period of serious illness which culminated in a hysterectomy. There was even a question at one stage of there being a malignant growth. She told me about this illness because during it she had a remarkable dream. In that dream she experienced a vision of hell, with thousands of voices pleading with God. She found herself calling out to discover where Jesus was. She then heard a voice which said simply 'She's mine.' The voice went on to assure her that he had been with her a very long time. When her husband and Father Peter came to see her soon after she had woken, she was still full of the wonder of a continuing sense of a presence of Jesus. They were somewhat less enthusiastic, ascribing it to the effect of the drugs.

A further experience followed, which Joan felt to be part of a process of being initiated into the total dimension of spiritual reality. It was an encounter with evil. As she describes it:

> Three nights after, I woke up in the middle of the night choking. I felt as though there was something so evil in that room and I didn't know what to do with myself. I had my rosary, my New Testament, and I began trying to say my rosary. But I was full of horror. So I opened my New Testament at random and found the end of Ephesians, all about principalities and powers of evil. This wasn't very comforting, but I look at it quite differently now and I think I was being delivered from something. I had written off Satan because I thought it was all psychological. I think that this was the Lord's way of showing me that it was real. It is significant because of what happens later.

Joan took the opportunity during convalescence to read extensively, and it was during her reading that she again experienced an enveloping presence of Jesus which led to her crying for the rest of the day with joy. She then felt the need to go right to the beginning of her Christian instruction, as a way of discovering how her experiences fitted in with Christian truth. Neither her husband nor Father Peter were taking her new enthusiasm for her faith with a great deal of sympathy. Her husband was a 'routine' Catholic, and Father Peter, as he told me later, did not understand religious experiences of this kind, being wedded to what he admitted was a rather traditional Catholicism. Joan's discovery of the gift of tongues was made in isolation, and it was some time before she recognized it for what it was. She explained:

> At first I couldn't make it out. Just before I went to sleep, I was just praying, loving the Lord really. I found that in prayer that I was using a whole new language. I even sat up in bed and thought: 'What am I saying?' It was yet another strange and beautiful experience. And yet as I drifted into sleep, this would persist. It was like bubbling water coming up from deep down within me. I have always thought of it as a language of love, because we have never got enough words of love, have we? Well, one day Les had flu, and I'd been praying downstairs and Les was suffering upstairs. Quite suddenly this tongue which I had kept for night use, as it were, began to bubble up, and I found that I was chattering away in a beautiful tongue. Something was so released in me that I felt that this must be for Les. So I went upstairs and said, 'You've got to come downstairs — I'm praying over you.' So

the poor dear man got out of his sick bed, staggered downstairs, and I prayed over him in my new-found release. He said afterwards that it was just as if he had got wooden railway sleepers all around him and they all fell down, he saw them all tumble down. And he started to want something, then his hunger began.

For Joan the discovery of the significance of these experiences came by chance two weeks later when they were visited by a Methodist couple they had known some five years. The couple shared with them a new and exciting spiritual experience they had had, and Joan was able to recognize in it the same thing as she had had. She began to want a prayer-group of her own, but it in fact started as the result of a visit of a missionary priest to the parish. Having talked with Joan, and seeing that she was anxious to begin, the priest unbeknown to her, encouraged three Spanish Carmelite nuns from a local convent to contact her. With Father Peter and her husband she had a ready-made prayer-group of six. They began to meet around January 1972, and it was not long before her husband also received the Baptism in the Spirit. Other members of the group also discovered the gift before the first year had passed. Joan described her husband's experience in this way:

We went to a Fountain Trust meeting in Birmingham and Les hearing Father Ian Petit speak. Les heard him right in here and, in the middle of that meeting, he was just caught up and filled with the Holy Spirit; he began to cry. Everybody cries I think. And so there were the two of us now.

The group, now supplemented by other denominations, Anglicans and Methodists, was now taking on an increasingly charismatic character. The healing aspect however only began in the autumn of that year. It was Joan herself, suffering from a bad back, who first received healing in the context of the group, when the members prayed for her. After this healing, new dimensions opened up for her and for the rest of the group. It was then that Father Peter and Joan went off to hear Francis MacNutt in Manchester speak about healing. This conference was to be decisive for Father Peter, as up to this point he had stood apart from the charismatic experience. He takes up the story:

In a parish a priest often has a place rather like Bethany where the Lord used to stay with the friends he liked. Joan and Les were in the parish, though on the very perimeter of it. I used to go down there on a Sunday evening to relax and let my hair down a bit. When there was this question of Joan starting this prayer-group, I was very much on the defensive. I was a cradle Catholic and I had been all through the whole normal mill, and all we could think of were the sacraments. You've got the sacraments, you've got it all nicely cut and dried. The book is there, and if you are in any difficulty you just find out what the Church teaches and that's it. Any sense of going beyond, and seeing that God works in other ways as well, that he is not just confined to the sacraments, didn't occur to me. When Joan told me about things at their early stages I was suspending judgement. Fortunately I wasn't writing it off. The Lord must have been protrecting me from that. I respected what she was saying because of my relationship with Joan. I knew she wasn't talking codswallop. I had trouble working out what this could be, and what relationship it could have with my Catholic faith. Then it came to this point when someone said why don't you go to Hopwood in Manchester. I went to Hopwood with Joan; it was an extraordinary experience for both of us. We were there five days and there was a tremendous lot of prayer and praise. There were a number of priests, about fifty, from all over the country, and we concelebrated mass every day; it was beautiful. Francis MacNutt invited us priests one day to a deliverance of a woman who had some evil. The laity were not invited because it was felt that many people who had come to this conference would be a bit shattered. It would have been a bit too strong for them. We saw this, and we saw what happened after he had prayed for this woman. There was a complete change in the personality of that woman even while he was praying. He had already done a lot of praying with her previously, but he knew that this was the culmination, this would be the final fling. I was being educated rather forcefully. So were the other priests. I didn't eat much lunch that day and Joan said I was white as a sheet. We didn't know what was going on; we didn't understand it at that time. There was also a dramatic healing in the lecture theatre, where the subject was 'healing', and the whole conference was present. MacNutt was discussing the ways and the importance of it, and that God can do all sorts of things. And then this lady was invited up on to the stage who had one leg shorter than the other. He started praying over the affected leg — she couldn't walk properly. He said, 'I want all of you to pray that the Lord may heal her, that she may be able to walk properly.' To this day I can't understand what happened, as it is almost too good to be true. He held this lady's leg in his hands, the short one, and as he was praying he said, 'It's now half an inch longer, now it's three-quarters of an inch.' And after twenty-five minutes — I testify to this that it wasn't an illusion, it wasn't magic or pretence — that leg was restored to the same length as the other. At the time I thought it was incredible. I thought, 'God really is working, he does work.' It was in prayer that it happened. The whole ambience was one of prayer. All those present were filled with, first, astonishment, and then utter wonderment. But a day or two after, in the afternoon when they used to have exposition of the Blessed Sacrament, I was kneeling quietly in the chapel with Joan. There were about forty people in the chapel but no one was leading any prayers. It was a quiet time of meditation. Suddenly I wanted to burst into tears. Then I wanted to laugh, and I began to shake. Something was happening to me and I wasn't too sure what was happening. Joan said, 'You had better come back'. I was afraid people would see me, because I was a bit self-conscious. One moment it was utter joy, the next minute it was weeping. I was in that state nearly forty-eight hours. I hardly slept a wink that night. I got up in the morning — people would say on an emotional high — but anyhow I started shaving and trying to keep control of myself. The next minute I burst into tears, and all the lather fell off and I had to start all over again. This went on well into the next morning. Then Joan said, 'I am going to ring the group at home — they've been praying for us while we've been away — to tell them the good news: Peter has received the Holy Spirit.' I believe I did. It doesn't happen with everyone like that in such a dramatic way. From that time onwards I saw everything in a different light. I was no longer sceptical. I changed. I was one of the last in the group to come into the experience. With all the other priests present, I knew it was not emotional blackmail, nor is it just emotion. I then began to think about theology, and realized that there is nothing here which contradicts. I was trying to stand apart and look at it, because I knew something had happened to me, but I had to be sure that it was on a sound basis.

Joan then commented:

This was eight months after the prayer-group had started, and in that time most of the people in the group had received the Baptism. One or two of the older ones never took that step. The ones who were really wanting had received, but you [addressing Father Peter] desired but your theology and your training had prevented it. But it came, thank God.

41

Father Peter continued with the story again. He told me how the Days of Renewal began. It had been Les whose energy got the whole thing going. For these Days, speakers from away were arranged, and publicity was given over the whole area. At the very beginning the three of them had seen these Days as primarily for the parish, with others coming in from outside. In fact, right from the beginning the outside element was predominant, and the attendance from the parish was fairly minimal. The local congregation, in spite of the fact that the Days of Renewal took place in their church building, never at any point took on board the new-found charismatic enthusiasm of their priest. There were no splits in the parish, since the two levels of ministry went on side by side. Father Peter did not appear to be either surprised or disappointed by this. What disappointment he might have felt at the lack of response from his parish was presumably more than compensated by the surprisingly large numbers who came for these services. The services appeared to be meeting a real hunger on the part of Catholics and others in the whole area around Stratford, Warwick and Coventry.

At the end of the Day the Eucharist was celebrated, and after it Les would invite up anyone who wished for prayer and laying on of hands for any need. Father Peter went on to explain what happened:

> I was doing this and there was one lady who had something very wrong with her neck. This was the first time we had this service. I put my hands round her neck and I prayed for her about two minutes. I prayed, 'May the Lord heal you', not something very powerful. And I had a letter from the lady afterwards which said, 'Thank you, Father, for praying over me. I'm completely recovered from my stiff neck.' I couldn't really believe at that stage that I was being used. Such was my hang-up. On the next Day of Renewal, someone came with a bad back. I put my hand on the small of her back. Well, blow me, I also heard within a day or two that that lady had been completely healed. It was something like curvature of the spine and it had gone. Then I said, 'Perhaps the Lord is using me.'

Joan took up the account in response to my question about whether they prayed separately or together at the Renewal Services:

Sometimes we prayed, the three of us, sometimes Les would call me to help him. We were being very much led by the Spirit. Sometimes one by one. We had no conscious plan at all. In fact we started our Renewal Days with no conscious plan. To our astonishment it jolly well worked. We found that there were three distinctive gifts we had. We discovered that Peter was good with physical healing, this is where it began to develop. But people came up with deep depressions, and though the Lord can do wonders, they needed to have a new understanding of themselves before anything could happen. And so we began to see people in our own home and pray with them, Les and myself. Sometimes Peter would come as well.

Father Peter added his own comment:

At that stage I sat quietly in the chair praying quietly while Joan and Les, one after the other or together, were praying, to reinforce it. We never thought of our ministry as being particularly Catholic, though lots of Catholics came to the Days of Renewal. They came from other parishes, and said: 'I wish we had something like this in our own parish.'

I then questioned Joan about the group again. How had it become a healing group? Was it a conscious decision on their part? Joan's answer was that they had begun as a straightforward prayer-group. But she went on to explain:

When the healing began, it was to our wonder and to our astonishment. It was at first very tentative. My back was healed without anyone laying a finger on me. We didn't touch each other in those days. We just said, 'Would you please, Lord, heal Joan's back'; but we were an incredibly loving group. Now it is the love that releases. We found that people were coming along within the group itself with problems. One of the first people that came to me personally to ask for my prayer said to me: 'Now you can't possibly know how I feel. I lost a baby in infancy. There is still this pain about it. Although it is all those years ago. And I feel a real anger still with God about it.' And I said: 'But I lost four children in infancy.' And I thought I had dealt with it satisfactorily. And it finished up that I got more healing than she did. But we were in it together. We were crying about our babies. And we decided that at that point we must give them to the Lord. And we both did this, and it was a tremendous healing for us both. This is what I mean about the love in a group where you can begin to trust each other with things like this, and this is really how it began to develop. And so people on Renewal Days came with deep wounds, and I believe it is more important to heal that, the psychological real hurts to the soul, than the physical, but they're so intertwined.

Father Peter came in at this point and commented, 'Joan has a strong gift of discernment, much stronger than mine. I just love people and pray for them and things happen physically.'

Joan went on to explain how the healing ministry developed at the beginning on two fronts and at several levels. First there was the healing going on in the group, as most of the members had something that needed healing. Then there were the individuals who were thrown up from the Days of Renewal. Every individual who came for healing from the Renewal Days enabled them to deepen their experience and their confidence. They had tried at the beginning to introduce individuals for healing prayer into the group sessions. Joan told me of one dramatic healing that had taken place through 'soaking prayer', to use a phrase from Father MacNutt's book. The woman concerned had arthritis, and after four meetings was completely cured, to the extent that her doctor declared that she had been mistakenly diagnosed. This kind of prayer within the group gradually ceased, as Joan and Les came to see that most individuals needed much personal counselling before the laying on of hands, and this involved the sharing of deeply personal information. Also the main problem thrown up from Renewal Days was that of depression and mental illness, or as she put it, 'hurts to the soul'. The group supported with prayer all that Les, Joan and Father Peter were doing, but it was becoming a healing ministry which began in the public services of renewal and was continued on a one-to-one basis. Joan recalled one particular example of someone who needed setting free from drug addiction:

> We had, bless her heart, a girl on heroin who came, and she was set free. She turned up one night in a terrible state. She had known my son at some point in her life, and she got married to someone he knew who had worked with him. She said could we do something to help. I took her up into my bedroom because she was in too much of a state to bring into the group. The group all prayed downstairs and I could hear them all singing; it was so reassuring. Well, I prayed with her and at that point her withdrawal symptoms left her. But I knew deep

in my heart, and this is where discernment comes in, that she wasn't cured. This was just a bit of an interval for her, a breathing space. She went off again, and I kept her in my prayer and I felt very concerned. She turned up about a month later. I just knew we had to do something practical to help her. So we took her in. Now I realize we were quite mad at the time. There should have been a crowd of people looking after her. We did it and we saw her through cold turkey. She had got the needle marks in her arm and we took it in turns to stay up with her. One night her arm was inflamed and hurting, and she was jerking about. She wouldn't go to her doctor, as she was frightened of the professionals completely. And Les just put his hand there and said, 'In Jesus' name, be healed.' And he took his hand away and there was smooth skin. And it shook her so much that she always held on to that when things got really bad. We learned a tremendous amount from her.

Joan then explained how their ministry had developed a new dimension, that of exorcism, or what she referred to as 'deliverance':

Les went to a meeting where some Anglicans had formed a prayer-group and they wanted someone to come and talk. He went there to help them establish this prayer-group. We all went on the first night. And they asked Les and someone else from the group to go for a number of weeks to help them. The second week when two of our group went along — I was in London — the local Vicar was there, a nice man. And the praise was really going, and it is in the praise that you see manifestations of the other chap, isn't it? And all of a sudden a lady rushed out of the room. Les thought she had heard her children crying, and thought nothing of it. After an interval her husband went off. He came back and got the Anglican priest and he went off. By now Les was wondering what on earth was going on. And then they came and asked Les. And it turned out that this girl had only been a Christian a short time. She had only been baptized a month or so before. It seemed that she had come from a family that were mixed up with a witches' coven. When he went upstairs, she said, 'I'm full of devils.' And he thought, 'What a strange lady', because once again it was a different language, so he thought, 'Well, she is just hysterical and a bit sick.' And then, he said, he looked at her and realized she was telling the truth. What was manifesting itself had been so threatened by her coming into the Lord and all the rest of it. So he and the Vicar were there the most of the night. We wouldn't have done the same a year or two later, but of course it seemed so important. We wouldn't have tired ourselves out. We would have

45

given some deliverance, let her rest, let us rest, build her up with prayer. But when he was thrown in like that he didn't know what to do. Anyway the Lord was very very kind. He really paved the way, the way he taught us was quite beautiful.

Up to this point I had listened to the account without expressing any surprise at what I was being told. Here I felt bound to comment on the fact that many people would find such a story unacceptable, and that their involvement in it was, on the face of it, foolhardy, and even dangerous. Joan accepted this remark, but it was quite clear that she trusted in the power of God to lead them and protect them and provide the means to deal with it:

It wasn't acceptable to us. But in healing we are involved with spiritual warfare. Until we are ready to handle it, we are not functioning fully. Someone has got to pick it up. We weren't looking for it. That was the first of many instances. Who was going to help that girl without deliverance? You have to recognize that first of all she needed deliverance. She had got something in her that was pulling her — she even looks different now. She has lost her burden. She could have gone to confession, she could have gone to a lot of things, and not have the freedom that she has got now. We have had two people who have been physically affected by their involvement with the occult. One person came from overseas on holiday and she was crippled up, and for want of a label they call it Disseminated Scelerosis. She had tunnel vision, and she had already had brain operations. She was in a terrible state. She was over here on holiday, and someone who knew my husband asked if we would see her, because she was even worse over here. I think she went to see a specialist in London. She turned up, and I found her repellent and I didn't know why. We began to pray with her, and I said to Les afterwards, 'There's something, there's something I feel that curdles within me.' He said the same. So the next time we saw her we looked at each other and he challenged whatever was there. And there was a manifestation and a real deep voice came out of that woman, and a snarl. We know that you cannot deliver if there is forgiveness needed, or self-knowledge. It is the truth setting you free really. So he said: 'Have you ever been involved in the occult at all?' She denied it vehemently. We pressed this, and it transpired that she had been involved in a Satan Club with some people in a psychiatric hospital — it sounds incredible, because she was one of the staff. This is a deliberate invitation to darkness. But they did it for kicks, and they thought it a bit of fun. She had some deliverance then, and it transpired that she was a lapsed Catholic. She needed a priest and we rang Father Peter up. For a cradle Catholic the clergy are the all-powerful ones; Father Peter was able to bring an authority to what was happening. She was delivered of something then, and her vision which had been tunnelled began to go right. But again we began to realize that she needed so much inner healing. Then it transpired that, when she had broken with this group, they had told her that she would be ill until she died. She had meningitis from a month later, so clearly they had got that sort of power. Through discernment we realized that she had got to be separated from this spiritual darkness, from the leader of the group on the other side of the world. We did that in prayer. She began to improve, and she went back to university. At first I was really nervous; it seemed as though the Lord really threw me in the deep end. These were not just mild neuroses, these were people that were deeply hurt — deeply infested. That first time we prayed I went to get the coffee and every cup was shaking. I though, 'I can't do it with this fear.' And I took myself away and put myself in the Lord, and I thought, 'No, it's your power.' And after that it was all right. It was my natural timidity, because after all we are naturally timid people. That's the funny part of it.

Joan went on to reflect on the particular contribution her husband had made in their healing and deliverance ministry. She felt that his own experience of suffering had given him a wonderful strength of love and compassion. He was able to demonstrate that love to uphold and sustain the most hurt individuals. And yet there was an ironical twist to this situation. Joan told me later that the hurts in Les' own life were, she believed, the cause of the cancer from which he died. Although he received much healing, Joan was never able to reach the depths of that hurt which she found to exist. There were, she believed, levels of hurt that were sometimes difficult if not impossible to reach. It was in that area that one must look if one wanted to explain why some received physical healing and some not.

I went on to ask Father Peter about his experience of healing and laying on of hands:

There is nothing dramatic about it. I just say, 'Lord, come into them.' It is strange, but I have an interest in anatomy and I can remember the names of the parts of the body. And I say, 'Lord, reign over that particular area, come into the very corpuscles of the blood, the nerve-endings. Whether that is necessary or not, this is how I do it. I think of the Lord going to the very focus of the trouble, rather than saying, 'I pray that they may get better.' It becomes more detailed. I am very conscious in exercising this ministry that I am not on my own. I feel the Lord is more likely to answer that prayer, when it is a community that is praying, whether that community is present or not. So when I am praying I am very conscious of Joan and Les praying, and also the prayer-group. It is not a matter of somebody coming out of the blue and my praying over them and they are instantly cured. It doesn't seem to work quite like that. When I pray with anyone who is sick, I am trying not to think of myself or even wondering why God uses me. I'm trying to think: 'Well, what a powerful thing prayer is, particularly for those who are hungry and thirsty for the Lord already, reaching out to him.'

I then asked Father Peter if he used tongues to pray with the sick. His reply indicated that he used them fairly often, though not inevitably:

When I pray in tongues I find my whole prayer is focused. Prayer has to be focused. Our old bidding prayer, 'Let us pray for the sick,' is not focused. With individuals you have to focus your prayer, specifically on them and on what is wrong with them. You have got to get rid of yourself and concentrate on what is wrong, and ask the Lord to work through you and use you, even though you are a weak vessel. 'These are not my hands, these are your hands. These are not my eyes, these are your eyes.'

Joan confirmed what Father Peter had said about the supportive prayer of the group. She and he both knew that they prayed every day, and especially for those who came for individual ministry.

Readers may have wondered how the ministry in Chipping Campden was received by the Diocesan Bishop. Joan told a moving story of how Les, on travelling to Bristol on business, had called and asked to see the Roman Catholic Bishop of Clifton. He was received late in the evening and talked to the Bishop for two hours about the events taking place in the parish. The Bishop's authority was needed, not so much for the healing ministry, but for the deliverance ministry that had begun. His reaction to Les's request was straight to the point. He simply quoted the passage of Scripture where Jesus responded to his disciples when they were complaining about others who were casting out devils in Christ's name but were not part of the group. Jesus's reply had been, 'Forbid them not.' 'That', said the Bishop, 'is what I say to you.' Both Father Peter and Joan felt that something remarkable had happened that night. They saw the hand of God at work in that event.

I asked Joan how she saw what she was doing in relation to the professional healers, psychotherapists and psychiatrists. Also I wondered how she saw prayer as a therapeutic aid in comparison with more conventional means:

Whatever I am doing, if it feels all right inside with prayer, then I have to go on with confidence. A dear soul came with the most awful migraine. It put her on her back for a week at a time. It was because this poor soul was trying to sit on a memory that she wasn't even aware of. But the more we prayed for her, the worse it became. We wondered, 'Are we doing any good?' Then I prayed about it, and we went on until finally the thing that she couldn't remember broke through. She was raped as a tiny child. Then we thought we were on winning ground. It was all coming out and a lot of forgiveness was tied up with it. But then, you see, she started to get worse again. We had touched on the memory side, her forgiveness and her grief, but then she had yet worse bouts of the migraine. Do you know what it was? It was very unexpected. Somehow the child had felt guilty about it although she was tiny. I think the guilt had been put on her by others. She had this terrible sense of badness and guilt. So we kept on bringing this little child with love before the Lord until she could do it herself. She was saying, 'Yes, yes. Poor child.' She was looking at herself objectively. And then the migraines went. That all took two years. First of all she could not admit to the memory being there in the first place. But we knew. She had been to everything and tried everything. It wasn't possible to heal that dear soul until she felt safe enough. I don't know really what happens. The memory is like a boxed-in thing which needs light shed on it. That is how I see it. There was a dark area that was causing all this problem. Until she was able to go there and look at it, and examine it and all the different facets of it, the forgiveness, the letting go of resentment and anger, she could not be healed.

'Sometimes people say, "I'll forgive but I'll never forget",' Father Peter commented; 'That is not forgiveness at all.'

Joan continued with another story about a boy called John with

49

whom she and Father Peter had been involved. This illustrated the way in which important insights were given to Joan while praying for people. These insights given to her through prayer often enabled the psychotherapeutic process to be greatly speeded up:

> John had had depression. He had received a certain amount of medical help, but it hadn't got to the root. He hadn't had psycho-therapy though. He came to us three times only. As I prayed with him it seemed that every time I mentioned his father — I pray where the Lord leads — his fist was clenched. I realized that there was so much anger against his father in him. His father had been away at war, and the little boy had grown up without him. He was so angry with his Dad because he had put him up as a kind of hero, but found when this hero came home that he had feet of clay. And so there was such a lot of anger in this poor boy, but he couldn't get to it. He didn't even know it was there. And so finally we got to the point where we said to him, 'Well John, you really are angry with him, you are so angry.' He was boiling, and he got to a point, as we were praying, that he was able to face it. It was as though the Lord gave him the strength to face what he was unwilling to face. And he started to hit the settee for all he was worth. And he got release, and there was this lovely moment of seeing his Dad with Jesus, seeing his Dad as lovable. He's been able to go up to his Dad and put his arms around him. He told us, 'I told him that I love him and we both cried.' So you see how the healing goes out beyond. He's married since then, and had a child. He found release once he got rid of the anger and that hurt. It was speeded up with prayer because it is the Lord who is doing the opening up. As he confronts people with their anger, with their resentments and their jealousies, he is the one who is going to help them to forgive, because you can't do it with your own strength. How can you forgive somebody who has raped you, when you are three or four years of age? How can you forgive them without that love on a human level? We are not capable of doing it. So this is where I think the speeding up comes. I am not trained. I just go along with the Lord. If you haven't had any training, or if you jump in without any sensitivity or without the Lord wanting you to jump in, you could do a whole lot of damage. Of course you could. So I do see the difficulty, and why people say this is dangerous.

Joan spoke further of how things were revealed to her by the postures that individuals adopted when she prayed for them:

As I pray for people, I watch them, because you give away so much with your body, I've found. You see the anger by the twitches here and there. It is as though there is another eye that is seeing things, that is registering. Again, this is all going on without much conscious thought. I listen and then I pray and I see where I am led. When we began to pray for one woman, she went into a foetal position, and said that she felt that her mother was trying to get rid of her. She felt pain and terrible grief. And that is when we began to get into this area. It baffled us at first. But once again we felt very strongly we had been led into this area. We felt quite happy about where we were. Going to hear Dr Lake, we heard it described, and that was very reassuring.

Sometimes you pray with a person and you know that they need to go somewhere but they can't do it — this is where the time comes in — I am willing to try, and keep on trying, if they are willing to have a go. Sometimes I am aware of the deep hurt or rejection in them, and I've got a fair idea of what happened to them — that is a kind of word of knowledge. But I can't do it until they are willing to go there, you see. Sometimes you find people will dive straight in there. Incidentally, women are far easier than men to pray with. They are far more open to prayer.

Joan found herself involved through her spiritual insight in the whole realm of birth and pre-birth trauma. She even found that some people were able to 'remember' their conception. This whole area, and the fearless way in which Joan and her husband were able to help in it, is a remarkable feature of this testimony. She was also aware of the dimension brought to people's attention in the book by Kenneth McAll, *Healing the Family Tree*; the capacity of one generation to hand on its psychic hurts to the next.

She went on to speak about the blocks that people put in the way of their own healing:

Real inner healing takes a long time, because people tend to spring back to their old attitudes. We found that unless people did their side, unless they were prepared to face the Lord, in opening their lives to the healing power of prayer, then we kept on sliding back to where we were before. We were going ten steps forwards and eight back. Every time they came back they'd still be in the same state of guilt. I sometimes have to plead with people to do something about their own prayer life. 'Oh, I will try', they say. It isn't like that, it is a matter of will, and you have to push their will. You are praying for the will and you are praying against the habit tracks. You so often have to go through layers of grief, rejection, anger and fear, like an onion. You have to work right down through the soul to the cause. It is very painful — painful to witness and painful for the person. Once they have gone through and they are praying people — and I do emphasize that — then they are going to hold on to that healing, with their memory healed by Christ.

The events of a thirteen-years' healing ministry that I have recorded are remarkable in themselves, but they are noteworthy in pointing to one particular truth. This is the fact that two lay-people with only the Spirit of God to guide them found themselves ministering to individuals with needs which would tax the most dedicated professional therapist. If we accept even a part of what has been recorded, it is clear that Joan and Les were, at a human level, remarkably gifted in discernment, and endowed with uncanny sensitivity. If one accepts their interpretation as to the source of these gifts, that the Risen Lord was guiding and working through them, then this is a testimony to that power. I myself was far more impressed with the fearless way in which they went on discovering new aspects of the healing ministry, when most people would have been tempted to hold back in sheer terror. Humanly speaking they could rely on no one. There was no 'expert' at the end of a phone to advise them. They needed and possessed immense reserves of courage and trust in the Risen Lord to have travelled so far down the road of discovering what healing power could mean in the world today.

The other point which came over strongly to me from the testimony of Joan and Father Peter was the immense amount of suffering in the world. The sensitivity of Joan in particular had opened my eyes to the sheer magnitude of mental suffering in human lives. Seeing the needs of others through her eyes and her compassion, was to have my imagination enlarged, and it is to be hoped that something of the immense compassion and love that Joan showed comes through the pages of this book. In their obedience to this call they have been able to show to all of us a glorious and triumphant simplicity and power which is given to those who trust and open themselves fully to God.

FOUR

The Healing Ministry of the 'Body'

The previous chapters of this book have been focused on a healing ministry exercised by individuals, whether or not they are linked with others who support them with prayer. The healing ministry of one particular Anglican priest, Roy Lawrence, and those who have been influenced by him, has a somewhat different emphasis. Roy puts forward an understanding of the healing ministry of the Church where there is no talk of gifts, but the whole congregation are involved, even if certain leaders, lay or clerical, exercise it in their name. There is an attempt to exercise a healing ministry which is an extension of the life and prayer of the whole congregation. Roy's story has something to teach us, not only about a ministry of healing, but also about the harnessing of parish life to this end.

Roy Lawrence has written two paperbacks on the ministry of healing, *Christian Healing Rediscovered* and *Invitation to Healing*, and these contain an account of how he first brought his parishes into this ministry, and how he and they have grown in their understanding of what is involved. Both these books are now out of print and this is to be regretted, since they contain much excellent material written from a standpoint that communicates itself by a total reasonableness and freedom from a narrow theological bias. The first of the two volumes contains an account of how Roy first came into a healing ministry. The original impulse was a conversation in a car, when it was pointed out that Jesus always linked preaching the gospel with the command to heal. This insight led Roy to make a special study of this theme during a sabbatical, and he then went back to his parish in Hyde in Cheshire determined to explore with the PCC and parish this important aspect of a pastoral and evangelistic ministry. For eighteen months he held services which were called 'Investigation into Christian Healing' on the first Sunday in the month. He records that while the quality of worship improved in his church, no physical healings in fact took place. It was then in 1974 that his parish took the step of inviting George Bennett, Warden of Crowhurst, the well-known Home of Healing, to come and speak. The service at which he was to speak was made the climax of a six-month mission, and was thrown open to all denominations in the area. The service was televised by Granada television and broadcast by BBC Radio Manchester. The visit of George Bennett had the effect of opening up a floodgate for them, and physical healings started to happen. The services of healing changed their name to 'Rediscovering Christian Healing'. Roy records in his book the additional detail that for a time after the mission all the leaders of the church simultaneously went through a period of spiritual darkness. It was as though they were under spiritual attack of some kind.

One noticeable feature of the healing ministry of Roy and his congregation, and also of Roy's own personal ministry beyond the parish, is that it has no bias of churchmanship like that which is normally found in a church with a strong sense of its own mission. The church at Prenton on the outskirts of Birkenhead where Roy now serves has the trappings of a middle-of-the-road parish with vestments and candles. He described himself to me as a 'gospel-centred Christian', but he added that Evangelicals found it very hard to decide whether he was an Evangelical or not. He claimed to preach a very simple gospel of the fact that Jesus makes a difference:

> By his crucifixion and his resurrection and his present availability to us, he can stand life upside-down, he can really make a difference. There is no substitute for a really personal relationship with him, no substitute for the salvation process in our lives. For me, salvation and healing are kindred words.

Because of this lack of a churchmanship label Roy found himself able to speak to many groups of all shades of opinion, from the Anglo-Catholic Pusey House in Oxford to a local Pentecostal gathering. In his relation to other Christians the only thing that he felt important for a full fellowship between them was a discernment that the reality of Jesus was present. But when some ecclesiastical shibboleth was given more importance than the Lord, then barriers started to arise. He hoped that for himself nothing in the Church was more important than Christ. When the Church did not centre itself on Christ, it offered not Christianity but idolatry. Clearly, though Roy did not say this, healing was a theme of gospel preaching that could and did transcend many of the old traditional barriers between Christians.

Roy made very clear to me a point which is raised in his book, namely that the gift of healing is given to a congregation rather than to an individual. The healer in every situation is Christ. This he felt was a point of difference from much standard charismatic teaching, where the gifts of the Spirit are perceived as being given to individuals. He mentioned that when he held services of laying on hands, there was not a longer queue in front of him than in front of the lay people and fellow clergy who assisted him. He went on to describe the services of healing that were held at Prenton:

We start off with a very ordinary evensong — ordinary in its format — and yet there is something in the air that is nothing to do with emotionalism, it's a blend of an acknowledgement of need and a sense of expectancy that God wills to meet our need. That's in the air, and it sharpens the sense of worship. Then we have a Bible study because we quite consciously try to see Jesus. The text I always have in my mind when I preach at a healing service is, 'Sir, we would see Jesus.' We look at Jesus in action, and during the singing of the hymn that follows we have the laying on of hands. Now this is administered by four of us working in two pairs. We administer to each other. Usually we get a clergyman and layman or laywoman administering together. The only qualification we reckon is necessary is belief. 'Those who believe shall lay hands on the sick, and they shall recover.' So we have to have people who believe in the Lord, believe in his healing ministry, and believe in the validity of its continuation through his Body the Church. On that basis we lay hands first on each other and then on any who come up to the communion rail. As we lay on hands we say in unison the little prayer, 'May the healing power of the Holy Spirit be in you.' So everyone who comes up has four hands laid on them, two pairs of hands. This is the Body of Christ giving the touch of Christ. It makes no difference whether I am laying on hands or not. At the next healing service I shall not be doing it. Two of my colleagues will be doing it and a man and his wife will be joining them.

Roy went on to stress that at a healing service, the individual was never asked what was wrong with them:

> The whole exercise is a practising of the presence of Christ. Our minds are on the Risen Lord. But in a one-to-one interview we would have quite a lengthy interview, when they would say how they feel and how life is with them. Then I would not do that very simple prayer. I would pray as would seem to be right when laying on of hands for healing of mind, body or life situation or whatever.

The exercise of 'practising the presence of Christ' is one of the most distinctive forms of healing prayer that Roy teaches. The congregation is led in an exercise of what might be called guided meditation, with a strong emphasis on visualization. In the so-called 'ring of peace', everyone is called to imagine themselves in the presence of Christ and sharing in his peace. That place of peace is also a place of healing, and the meditator is then invited to place there first his family, then those known to be in need of any kind. Gradually the ring of peace extends further and further outwards until it encompasses the neighbourhood, the country, and finally the world. When I interviewed Roy he had recently come back from a workshop in healing prayer in which this particular method had been taught and put into practice. Along with this method other forms of guided meditation were experienced by the participants, most of which are dealt with in his second book. But the final method of healing prayer which he recounted to me does not appear in his writings, so I quote his words in full as a way of giving the flavour of Roy's understanding of meditative prayer:

> The fourth thing that we did was a session entitled 'Praying with Jesus'. He said, 'When you pray, say this', and he taught us the Lord's Prayer. It was one of my colleagues who pointed this out to me, that to pray the Lord's Prayer as an act of leisurely and gentle meditation for oneself and then for other people — this is a marvellous experience of healing prayer. It's all there — the things that we need, the healing relationship with God which is of the essence of Christian healing. If God is the supreme being, then a relationship with him is supremely healing. And so one starts off with that in the word 'Father'. We have it corporately, and so you have not just 'Father' as in St Luke, but 'Our Father' as in St Matthew. And as you go through the Lord's

Prayer clause by clause, each clause tells us something about the nature of Christian healing. 'Who art in heaven' reminds us that God's nature is of the highest and the best. To acknowledge God as God is to practise the very essence of positivity — it is to acknowledge the worth and the value of all that we know to be highest and best. It is to feed our minds on that which is essentially true and good, and we are what we feed on. Very often we feed on garbage in spiritual terms, so to say the Lord's Prayer and to ponder that phrase is a healing act, and so it goes on. Each clause in it leads further into the ministry of Christian healing. So you do it for yourself first and then you do it for somebody else — you lay the Lord's Prayer on somebody else and you do them good as you do so. It is quite something to have that kind of experience of a workshop of healing prayer. It is not only a lecturer imparting what is in him but everyone shares what is in them, and you do have a convergence of various insights of the truth.

The practice of these forms of meditative prayer was part of the way in which Roy saw whole congregations playing their part in the healing ministry. He spoke of a sense of relief that he was not someone with a special 'gift'. When such gifts existed in a congregation, then it tended to let others off the need to do anything about it. He thought that his particular ministry of encouragement and infecting others with the importance of taking healing seriously would be less effective if he were perceived to be gifted either psychically or charismatically. He repeated his belief that the ministry was that of the Body:

> The Body of Christ is meant to be identified with Christ himself. Christ had various ingredients in his life which were not dispensible but were part of his essence. Healing was one of those ingredients. If we are the Body of Christ we must have a healing purpose, and if I am a professional representative of that Body then I would be untrue to the Body that I represent unless I took the whole ministry of healing seriously. The only healer that needs to be present at my healing service is Christ. We are practising this presence.

Roy stressed more than once how he began his ministry as an act of obedience to the command of Christ. Once he had grasped this command then he began to see how much of basic Christian doctrine was concerned with the matter of man's wholeness, both spiritual and physical. A crucial idea which he stresses in his book, and which sums up clearly why healing is so important in the context of normal Christian belief, is what he calls the Trinitarian basis of the ministry. His words on this theme are worth quoting in full, because, in their simplicity and directness, they make it hard for anyone to argue against the centrality of healing in any presentation of the Christian gospel:

I would think of the theological resources for Christian healing as being essentially Trinitarian. If we believe in God the Father, whose essence is creativity, then how must the spirit of creativity react when it comes across something that is as damaged as this world and the people in this world? Logically it must show itself as a spirit of recreativity. So if we believe in God the Father and put ourselves in the hands of God the Father when we ourselves are damaged, then God's influence on us must be recreative. So God the Father and all that we believe about his creativity is a basic element in our theology of healing.

God the Son leads us to a theology of healing. As Jesus went about, he found himself inevitably healing all manner of sickness and disease among the people. Just look at it statistically. In what percentage, when people came up to him and asked him for healing, did Jesus offer them the ministry of healing, and in what percentage did he say 'No, go away, this suffering has been sent to you by God for your ennobling?' In the first case one hundred per cent and in the second case nil per cent. If we take it that Jesus is in some sense our window into God, that shows us his attitude to the whole concept of the need for healing. And not only do we have the example of Jesus from the past but we have got his promise that 'Where two or three are gathered together in my name, there am I in the midst.' To worship is not to commemorate a dead Jesus, it is to meet a living, risen Jesus Christ. He is the same, the same yesterday, today and for ever, the same Jesus who found it inevitable to go round touching people with new wholeness. And this is so not only within the experience of corporate worship. Christian life is supposed to be a walk with Jesus — 'Lo, I am with you always, even to the end of the world.' If to be a Christian is to be with the living Christ, and the living Christ found that inevitably he went round touching people for wholeness, then to take Jesus Christ seriously is to take contemporary Christian healing seriously. But then we are not only to experience him, we are to convey him to others; hence his command to every disciple to preach and heal. That's a command that comes to us all. It's all part of our belief in God the Son.

And then there is God the Holy Spirit. If we believe in God the

58

Holy Spirit, if we believe that God not only wills to be around us but also within us, if we take the promise of Jesus seriously that God the Father will give the Holy Spirit to those who ask him, and if we ask for the Holy Spirit in the name of Jesus, then we can take the Spirit's activity within us for granted. So if we have some kind of God presence within us, and the Holy Spirit is the Lord, the giver of life, the fact of God within us must be gently nudging aside things in us — and we all have them — that are alien to life at its fullest and its best and its most whole. As the Spirit moves in us, he's moving with new life, and he is moving to the exclusion of those things that are alien to God's life and purpose within us. So if we believe in God the Father, God the Son and God the Holy Spirit, we believe in the resources for the ministry of Christian healing.

Roy spoke these words with great fluency and conviction, and it was evident that this piece of teaching was used by him on many occasions. Such a clarity of vision, unqualified by reservations of a theological or practical kind, makes him a powerful apologist for the Christian healing ministry across a wide range of Christian traditions. The experience of the ministry of healing had simultaneously placed him at the point where he knew and experienced the power and activity of God, and had burnt out any exclusiveness in his theological position. It is as if healing and all that it implies had brought Roy to the point of true ecumenism, a position of total openness to other Christians without any woolliness in his Christian experience. There was nothing in Roy of the fear and defensiveness that is a feature of so many Christians who claim to be preserving truth. Truth, if it is really God's truth, does not need our protection, it only needs proclamation. But the wonderful feature of a ministry of healing is that it is not just the proclamation of words, but also of works, and thus it is close to the ministry of Jesus himself. In summing up my impression of Roy I would note some definite 'charismatic' facets, even if he is not formally linked with this network. But he is joined to them in his total confidence in the Lord's will to heal, and in his expectation of the power of the Spirit of God to be at work among his people. I noted one small but significant point about Roy when he was talking to me about the various missions he had led around the country. He told me that he did not use a prepared script in the addresses that he delivered at these missions. This fact of reliance on the Holy Spirit, together with the obvious impact of his missions that I had heard from other sources, left me in little doubt that a recognizably charismatic impulse inspired his approach both to preaching and to healing. Perhaps we can recognize in Roy's ministry a style that belongs to the future. It is a style that is charismatic yet in no way divisive, ecumenical and broad yet not woolly, Church-based yet in no way sectarian, and finally it has achieved a pattern of leadership in apparent total harmony with colleagues and congregation. I might go so far as to say that Roy points us to a pattern of ministry which is not just directed at broken individuals; he also moves towards the healing of many of the divisions and broken-nesses of church structures and life.

Among the names of places and people that Roy was in touch with around the country he mentioned the parish of Gateacre, near Liverpool, and its team Vicar of St Mark's, Childwall Valley, Neil Cosslett. I wrote to Neil and we eventually arranged a meeting at the end of July 1984. Before this Neil had made it possible for me to attend a conference for lay people of the Liverpool Diocese at Swanwick on the topic of Healing. Neil was acting as chaplain. It was a strange experience for a clergyman to move around incognito among three hundred laity from another diocese. I welcomed the opportunity to attend the conference for several reasons. One was the reputation that the Liverpool diocese has gained in the whole realm of healing, with one in three parishes said to have a healing ministry of some kind. Also, Liverpool had produced a report of a working party in 1981 on the subject of healing. It promised to be a lively conference. In the event I was a little disappointed. Anglican caution on the matter on whether healing actually happened came over to the audience in some of the main addresses. I particularly remember a question to an eminent consultant who was part of a panel. He evidently believed in the possibility of healing, but he had never witnessed it. One felt that there were not enough people around in the conference who had had incontrovertible experience of the reality of healing to encourage the others who were just beginning. I found myself reassuring several people who were seeking encouragement on this very point. I also got the impression from talking to individuals that while there were many healing services going on in the parishes, many incumbents were not very confident in what they were doing. I may possibly have misjudged the mood, but this was what I came away with. In contrast, the charismatic parishes that were represented had obviously moved much further ahead. I should add that I only questioned some eighteen people out of the hundred-plus parishes represented there. I did however wonder whether this impression might not be typical of other parts of the country as well.

Neil Cosslett's role as chaplain meant that he did not speak at any length to the Conference until the final service of healing, which he led. The sense of peace and confidence that he spread throughout the congregation at this service was remarkable. The anecdotal material which he brought into his address, connected with his experience of healing, filled up what had been up to that point lacking in the content of the conference. It showed him to be a man of prayer, at home in a wide variety of pastoral situations and able to cope with every kind of human need. I looked forward to my meeting with him, and carried away a typescript of his forthcoming book, *His Healing Hands*, to study before our interview.

The book I have just mentioned contains much if not most of what Neil believes about the healing ministry. The remarks that I make here can perhaps do something to fill out the context of his work and re-emphasize the main priorities that he sees. For the outsider the most striking aspect of the context of Neil's work is the physical setting of his parish. His church and Vicarage stand surrounded by vandal-proof railings in the middle of the only large green area on a somewhat unexciting council estate on the outskirts of Liverpool. Coming from the countryside of Herefordshire, I found the boarded-up shops, graffiti and air of decay rather oppressive. Neil spoke not just of the vandalism but also of the sheer inertia that descends on people faced with unemployment and poverty. Little of this comes through in his writing.

The other context of Neil's ministry is the whole spiritual atmosphere which pervades the congregational life of his parish. I was not of course able to participate in any of Neil's services except the one at Swanwick, but it was clear to me that he moved in what was recognizably a charismatic atmosphere. He told me how he had gone to the Post-Green Community for a minister's course. Here he received a charismatic experience of brokenness and Baptism in the Holy Spirit. For him that first experience was not a once-for-all experience, he had received other experiences of blessing. 'Filling with the Holy Spirit happens again and again,' he told me. He admitted that he had played down the charismatic dimension in his book, because, as he put it, 'I want people to find their way into things charismatic in a very gentle way, like I did.' He went on, 'If you come into our church, people don't wave their hands about — one or two might — but nobody is expected to.'

Roy Lawrence's ideas of the healing ministry's belonging to the Church and not to him as an individual were strongly supported by Neil:

> I believe that God has a corporate gift of healing available in every church and I believe that is backed up by Scripture — the commissionings, go out and preach and teach. This is my personal view, and I believe that unless there is a real atmosphere of believing prayer and a real atmosphere of love you can forget it. There is also a time for acting as a priest alone, though I'd rather take other people, but now and again there is a situation where you just have to do it.

Neil's sense of the corporate nature of the healing ministry in the parish is not just an idea, but is worked out in a very practical way in the running of the parish. The full-time staff consist of Neil and a Church Army Captain, Dave Florence. There is also a group of nine people who are a pastoral ministry team but are known as an 'Elder Group'. This group meets every other Sunday and monitors all aspects of ministry, including healing. Neil told me that he allowed this group to act as a check or guide on himself and Dave. He found no difficulty in sharing all the problems of ministry with this group, and they in turn shared with him. He saw his role as an apostolic one. 'I'm trying to establish a leadership so that it will run without me. I'm to be here for a time, to lead for a time and to go for a time', he told me. 'A tremendous number of clergy', he observed, 'feel threatened by sharing.'

Beyond the elders are the area group leaders. At the heart of the praying life of the parish are the members of the Fellowship

Group, which meets on alternate Wednesdays with an average attendance of around twenty. Neil recalled how at the beginning of his healing ministry he was forced to go to members of his congregation for prayer support to face crisis after crisis that arose. The prayer support group would be contacted by phone to pray him and his colleagues through a crisis.

Every three months a Healing Service is held in the parish. When they take place Neil and Dave are supported by some of the elders, so that there are two teams of three ministering at the altar rail. Neil also mentioned that when he went to other churches to minister he would take two of his elders with him as support. Sometimes in cases of more serious illness he would use anointing oil, but he had no fixed policy about this. Before the service there would be a time of prayer for those involved in the laying on of hands, and they would commission each other for the ministry. Neil went on to talk about the visual imagery that he found helpful when praying for the sick. He told me that a former colleague 'believed that when you were praying with people you focused on them and their illness and pictured them better. My way was to focus on Christ — I'd look at the person and then I'd let them out of my mind and I'd focus on Christ's hands — and in my mind I'd picture his hands touching that person.' He went on to quote Roy Lawrence, who had said, 'You mustn't get yourself tied up in the troubles of the people who come forward, otherwise you will burn yourself out.' He continued, 'I don't believe in looking at problems — you look at the power to heal, and that is why I pray in the way I do.'

I was privileged to hear from Neil the story of how his book, *His Healing Hands*, came to be written. It is a story that helps to give something of the atmosphere of Neil's ministry and work:

> We have a lady with prophetic gifts. In our Tudor room, our little back room, we were having a healing service. We were just getting going and she had a little picture of a book in her mind. She felt it meant that she had to go and get that book. She thought it was called 'The Healing Hands of God'. And so she went off round all the shops and couldn't find the book. Then she told me about it. She was very puzzled. I said, 'It doesn't make any sense to me — perhaps it's going to be published soon.' So we left it, and it was about three years later when I was thinking about Sabbaticals when she came and said, 'I've

got the rest of the message — you've got to write the book.' I laughed, and I said, 'I can't write the book, I'm not a writer.' She said, 'Well, that's the message, you're supposed to write the book.' I was going to write something on the charismatic movement, but then as I thought about it I realized that I wasn't qualified to write on that, but I began to realize that I did know quite a bit about healing, and if I did a lot of reading, I'd know a lot more.

Neil went on to tell me how he eventually finished the book and sent it off to Edward England by second class post one Monday morning. He received an acceptance on the Wednesday following. In view of the success the book has been, the judgement made instantly by Edward England and later by Hodders was amply justified. Neil felt all the way through writing it a tremendous fluency, as though the Holy Spirit was guiding him at every stage.

Neil's final observations about the ministry of healing are tremendously important, and were re-echoed over and over again by the people I spoke to:

The mistake I made at the beginning was to think that the healing ministry is something that you do on your own ability, knowledge and strength. That's a disastrous mistake. You do it in your weakness and your total dependence on Christ. That's how I started — I didn't feel good enough, equipped enough, well enough, and it's a load of rubbish. You don't need to be all that. You just need to be weak and to lean on God.

He went on to say how important the experience of actually being ill with cancer had been in developing his ministry. 'Perhaps I made the biggest jump in the healing ministry through the cancer, learning more and more about myself. I had to learn from the other side; you can't just learn from the ministering. I had to experience being ill, the feelings, how you react . . .'

Neil told me in the course of our conversation about various examples of healings not included in his book, but I have thought best not to include them as they don't add anything to what he recounts in his book. What I have included here stands on its own, but also fills out some aspects of Neil's own written account about his ministry. I hope that the moderation as well as the tremendous wisdom and power of Neil's writing and ministry will achieve the recognition in the Church that they deserve.

Roy Lawrence and Neil Cosslett between them have well expounded a particular approach to the healing ministry which may ring true for many of my readers who are wary of the talk of gifts, miracles and charismatic exuberance. Roy's ministry of evangelism and his encouragement for the healing ministry have taken him all over the country, and many have heard his message. It must not however be assumed that the message of the importance of the healing ministry has been welcomed with instant acclaim everywhere he has gone. The impression I have gained is that the challenge given by Roy has turned out to be too strong for many of his listeners, who at the time may have 'heard him gladly'.

One area Roy visited was the Swansea and Brecon Diocese of the Church in Wales. Roy conducted what he felt to be a worthwhile mission there in 1981, to both halves of the diocese. Living only two hours away from Swansea, I decided to see how Roy's encouragement for the healing ministry had been received by the ordinary parish. Through the good offices of the Diocesan Missioner, Arthur Howells, I was privileged to meet two parish priests who, it appears, alone in the Swansea area had picked up Roy's challenge to begin a ministry of healing in the context of their parish life. Neither story is spectacular, but the sheer ordinariness of their accounts may be an important counterbalance to the 'successes' described in other parts of this book. It may also help anyone who recognizes the compelling correctness of Roy's message to see possible difficulties involved in setting up a healing ministry within the parish context.

Ivan, the first of the two priests, explained to me first of all something of the impact that Roy's visit had made on him and his parish three years previously:

> The healing ministry, as far as I'm concerned, started when Roy Lawrence came to Swansea. He was using our church for an archdeaconary service, and after we'd had a meeting in the morning with the clergy, and a few lay people as well, he said to me, 'Of course you will help me with the laying on of hands this evening.' Never having done anything like this before, I said, 'No way.' And he said, 'Yes, please, this is a normal part of the ministry of the Anglican church and they want you to help.' He was the sort of personality that

if he told you you ought to be doing something, you felt you ought to do something. He's got a quiet sort of authority. He said the same to Christine, my deacon, and she was equally perturbed. And yet she felt that because he told her that it was something she must do, she must do it. And so the evening came, it was glorious. About three hundred people came, there was a lovely atmosphere and it was so simple. The fact that it is Anglican is important. People have been brought up to this sort of atmosphere and they need something that relates to their experience. That evening there must have been fifty or sixty people from the parish who came — partly out of curiosity and partly because I had persuaded them to come. It was a beautiful service. And I didn't feel anything with the laying on of hands. And yet I felt when it was finished that here was something that had started, that God had pushed me into a corner as it were, and that we must go on from here. On the Monday morning when I met Christine, she felt the same thing; this was something that had to go on. Roy Lawrence underlined the fact that it was to be a normal part of the ministry of the Church — Jesus had said, 'Teach and heal'. We couldn't find any way out of that. There was no way I could say, 'This is not for me'. Everything had seemed so logical and so sensible. So we decided we'd carry on — a week-night once a month. So it would be the third Tuesday in the month. We've never had more than thirty-five present and it can perhaps be as low as twenty. This has gone on for over two years now. I talked to the Church Council about it, I talked to the people about it following his visit, saying, 'You have experienced something, how do you react?' There was a positive sort of reaction from a number of people, and it was felt that if this was something that we did, there would be sufficient people in the parish that would come along.

Ivan mentioned that his parish had a small prayer-group. This group had been involved with a woman who had had breast cancer, and as a group they had laid hands on her before Roy Lawrence's visit. The woman had died three months later, but her death was painless and peaceful, and they had taken this as an encouragement. The prayer-group naturally welcomed Roy's visit, as here was someone who was telling them the direction in which they should go. Naturally the prayer-group had been an important part in the inauguration of the healing services. In contrast, Ivan spoke about a great deal of suspicion and fear on the part of most of the congregation. The fear of the congregation reflected his own fear, particularly at the beginning, that nothing was going to happen. But the obedience to the command of Jesus enabled him to go on. He mentioned the story of Barbara, whose husband had left her. She was filled with a great bitterness which she was enabled to share with Ivan. At a healing service Barbara asked God to take away her bitterness. The bitterness was removed, but in its place was a great emptiness and depression. At the next service Barbara asked God to give her something to replace the emptiness she was experiencing. In its place she received an incredible sense of peace and joy. The importance of Barbara's experience was that she was ready to share it with the whole congregation, and she spoke for twenty minutes, making any other address redundant! This event encouraged Ivan at an early stage that the ministry was being blessed.

Ivan told another story, of a woman who had come to the healing service with deafness. She had given up being the secretary of a Church Council because of the deafness. The hospital gave her a hearing aid to use until such time as she would be completely deaf. She spoke to Ivan on the Tuesday after the service. "'It's embarrassing," she said, "because I don't need to use my hearing aid any more. I haven't told anyone else yet — I can't tell my son.'"

But in spite of this embarrassment the woman had gone on to tell many people what had happened, and was quite convinced that it was the healing service that had helped her. Ivan also spoke of a woman whose headaches disappeared over a period of months. The woman concerned had never asked for healing for herself, but always for others, and so it was something of a surprise to her to find that her own problem had vanished.

An interesting result of the healing services was the effect on Ivan's overall pastoral ministry. People, he found, were much more open after a healing service. He told me:

> I think they let you see a bit more of themselves on condition that you let them see a bit more of yourself. I have shared with them, in some of the healing services, my doubts and my uncertainties about it.
> This has helped them to open up with me, because they can see that I am doing this not because I wanted to do it but because God pushed me into a corner.

I also asked him about the effect on his prayer life:

I don't talk so much when I'm praying. I find that silence is a lot more attractive than it used to be. It is something that is affecting the Church and it is something that people are beginning to ask for in the worship of the Church. On Sunday morning in the Prayer for the Church there was a pause — for a few minutes I suppose — and there wasn't the normal fidgeting. And perhaps it is because I am learning to be a bit quieter.

The second priest, Douglas, spoke of a tentative interest in the healing ministry before Roy Lawrence's visit. His training at Mirfield had taught him about the sacrament of unction, but his recollection of this was that it was to be administered sparingly and only on request. He recalled an incident in his first curacy, which he had never talked about before, with a woman dying of cancer. He had taken a lot of trouble in preparing himself for administering the sacrament of unction, with prayer and fasting. Her subsequent deterioration and death discouraged him from repeating this, though he continued to bless his sick parishioners through touch. One woman in his second curacy apparently responded to this prayer and touch, and told him that he had healing hands. This encouraged him in a ministry of blessing the sick, but it was not until Roy Lawrence's visit that he took it any further. With Roy's visit he began to preach and teach in his parish as far as he could the basic fact that the Church has an obligation to do what Christ has commanded. Preaching and healing go together. Douglas's problem in setting up a healing service was that, though he believed in the importance of having a colleague to share the laying on of hands, his people, belonging to a parish that was, as he put it, 'very priest-ridden', would not accept a lay person laying on hands. He got round the problem by inviting Arthur Howells to share in the ministry until he eventually received a curate.

Douglas, like Ivan, had been greatly helped by the existence of a prayer-group, which had providentially come into being just before Roy Lawrence's visit. It was this group that took on the task of studying Roy's books and generally being taught about the healing ministry. Douglas encouraged them to come early before the healing services to pray for a quarter of an hour, but this backfired slightly when the sight of people praying at the altar rail inhibited the rest of the congregation entering the church. It was then decided that it would be better if they prayed in their normal seats in church. The healing services normally took place on a Sunday evening after evensong. These services attracted between sixty and seventy people instead of the usual ten to fourteen at normal evensong. Unlike Ivan, Douglas was not able to point to any dramatic healings, though he recalled a rather surprising event that took place early on, when a couple, living together but unmarried, attended. Through the service both were totally converted to Christ. The result was that they went off immediately to get married, though they did not stay with Douglas's congregation. He imagined that they had found their way to a charismatic church.

In spite of no dramatic healings, Douglas spoke of the changed atmosphere of worship:

> One of the encouragements is that we do get a tremendous sense of expectancy which we don't seem to find at other services. You keep telling your people that God is active, and that they must expect him to be active in the worship and in the Church. But they come there, they sit there and go to sleep, but they don't expect anything to happen. 'What happened at church this morning?' 'Oh the Vicar preached and that was that.' Whereas these healing services do seem to have a tremendous sense of expectancy about them, and people have commented about this. They have said it is a pity that we can't get this same sense of expectancy in all our worship. The fact that there is something different happening is important. We Anglicans tend to be hide-bound by our system, and we're afraid to go berserk now and then and to change things.

The witness of Ivan and Douglas to the Church's ministry of healing in a somewhat isolated context is of great interest to our survey. Both were finding congregational resistance, albeit of different kinds, and both were having repeatedly to reassure themselves of the rightness of what they were doing when things were not easy. Their witness for the healing ministry of the Church would be still more effective if they were not being subtly undermined by the problem of their isolation from other churches engaged in the same ministry. Also Neil Cosslett's words about the need for an 'atmosphere of believing prayer and a real atmosphere of love' remind us of the difficulty that a church of any tradition will have in setting up an effective ministry through healing services. It will only be a minority of churches that can provide such an environment. The road to achieving it will be full of problems and pain, as Christians learn to love one another and overcome their innate tendency to seek power and glory for themselves even at the expense of their fellow Christians. The 'Kingdom' in which the healing power of God is known and experienced demands a great deal of mutual forgiveness and repentance before it can be glimpsed in the ordinary parish context. Roy Lawrence, by pointing to the vocation of the whole Church to be the agent of healing in the world today, is also pointing the Church to its true vocation to be the embodiment of the Kingdom. What more costly and difficult task could be set for a church congregation? But it is in struggling to be an expression of God's kingdom and a focus of healing power that the church congregation is in fact moving to be its true self.

FIVE

Healing Doctors

The attitude of the medical profession towards healing is, perhaps predictably, cautious. Many doctors are impressed with the help offered by the Church and others in the area of healing and laying on of hands. But they remain cautious because what is happening in these cases appears to have nothing to do with the science in which they were trained. Without a framework of understanding they are restricted in what they feel they can say about it. They neither want to forbid it, nor be seen to encourage it in case the scientific framework of their training is seen to be in any way under threat.

The two doctors whom I have interviewed for this chapter come from two very different backgrounds. Both are however able to overcome whatever restraints their training might have put on them by being brought face to face with the fact of healing. Thus their medical knowledge is reconciled with the very different form of knowledge gained from the experience of healing. Dr Ian Pearce firmly accepts a holistic approach to medicine, and we shall be looking further at the philosophy of this approach in a later chapter. His perspective is also a Christian one, but he has a Christianity which has been affected by some of the alternative spiritualities that are around. In contrast, the second doctor is more in the mainstream of Church life. Her comments are still challenging, both to the medical and Church establishments. She has asked to remain anonymous for obvious reasons. She and Dr Pearce help to present the fact of healing from a medical, albeit unorthodox, perspective, and one hopes that their ready acceptance and practice of healing will be shared by an increasing number of their medical colleagues in the years that lie ahead.

Dr Pearce is well known as a writer and lecturer in the field of healing and cancer. His recent book, *The Gate of Healing*, is a good survey of much of the current thinking in holistic medicine and its application to cancer in particular. I met him one afternoon in the early summer of 1984, when he was staying at a caravan-site in the Forest of Dean. I began our conversation by asking him about his Christian background. He explained that he came from impeccable Anglican stock, his father a Canon of Durham and an uncle and aunt both in the mission field. His school education had been at Lancing, in his day in particular a High-Church Anglican public school.

The event that led him into healing and his whole interest in holistic medicine was the death of his only daughter, then in her twenties, from leukemia. He explained,

> I was pushed down a psychic pathway which I hadn't set out to travel down at all. In consequence of this I came into contact with the man who was the then administrator of the National Association of Spiritual Healers. He showed me concrete evidence that non-physical healing was an indisputable fact and not a fantasy.

Dr Pearce evidently had some experiences of a psychic kind which went outside anything he had known before. I did not press him about what actually happened, but quite clearly they were sufficiently important to change his whole life and the whole direction of his practice of medicine. It is noteworthy that he felt able to relate these experiences better to someone outside the Church with experience of the whole realm of the psychic and what we have referred to as natural healing.

His initiation into the experience of healing came about in an almost casual way:

> One day a woman came into my surgery with a lump in her breast. And for some reason while I was examining her, I tried to make a mental link and communicate some healing through my hands without telling her what I was doing. I then referred her off to the surgeon as any GP would do — urgent case, et cetera. Three weeks elapsed before she got her appointment. At the end of this I got a delightful letter from the surgeon whom I knew well. It said: 'Dear Ian, I don't know what you are alarmed about; there is nothing in this woman's breast.' The thing had disappeared. I was far too experienced at that time in my career to have confused a transient condition, a cyst or

something like that, with the genuine lump. I knew it was genuine. When I spoke to Gilbert (Anderson of the National Association of Spiritual Healers) about it, he said: 'Yes, this is the way things happen. They' (whatever that may mean) 'will often ensure you get two or three spectacular things like that to wake you up.' And in fact two or three things all happened in a relatively short space of time.

It is clear that Gilbert Anderson interpreted Dr Pearce's healing experiences in spiritualist terms. He himself was somewhat dismissive of this claim as far as he was concerned, though clearly a 'spiritual' terminology has to some extent coloured his thinking:

Many people claim to have discarnates working through them, but this is a delusion on their part which fits in with their spiritualist beliefs. The discarnate is a convenient peg of dissociation from the material. If one is to heal one has to switch off — like meditation — a dependence on the material world and the material senses around, and I think this is probably the way they use to do it. You and I when working will use a different method, through prayer, through an attempt at personal subordination of ourselves, to turn ourselves into a perfect channel.

Dr Pearce had little time for this spiritualist interpretation of Gilbert Anderson's. In fact the original experience that had led him into healing had deepened his Christian faith, and he claimed the Eucharist to be very important to him. But his Christian faith remained by orthodox standards slightly esoteric. He told me:

I also use meditation. I started off by being taught Transcendental Meditation, of all things. I moved on from that, realizing that there are — obviously one started to read — as many methods of meditation as there are meditators. TM was one technique, and quite a good technique for the person who has no spiritual beliefs or insights at all. But for me it had to move beyond that.

I then asked him whether the Church had played any part in his spiritual quest; he replied simply, 'The Church gave me no guidance at all. That is the tragedy of it.'

We need to ponder this remark a moment, and note that it was not meant as any kind of attack on the Church, which in other respects he valued more than ever. It was merely a sense that in this spiritual adventure he had begun, some of the old categories of thought that were part of his church life were simply not broad enough to contain his new experience. It is quite clear that within the Church of England at any rate a whole range of advice would have been forthcoming if he had known where to look. Much of the advice would have been hostile and condemnatory of the experience, while other viewpoints would have been more sympathetic. I myself on the day of the interview felt totally unable to comment on the value or otherwise of this experience, and I imagine that many of my fellow clergy would have been equally nonplussed by it. Are we to be so surprised that Dr Pearce found his way to a group who were ready to recognize and evaluate, albeit on their own terms, the experience he had had? His ambivalent attitude towards the Church was also clear when I asked him about his current spiritual practice. Clearly the teaching of spirituality was not thought by him to be high on its agenda. Can we really say that he is wrong? He said:

> It varies from one day to another. I still use the mantra I was taught, and I use — and I find this most potent of all — the so-called 'Prayer of the Heart', the Jesus Prayer which is part of the Eastern Orthodox tradition. Eastern Orthodoxy has never cast aside the practice of meditation in the way the Anglican Church has done. It seems to be disregarded even among the priesthood. When I heal, I am trying as far as possible to still the restless mind so that no thought is passing at all. What helps is music, music of a particular kind. My attention is focused on it, and it helps to still the mind. I try to see myself as an open chalice for a power that is beyond.

Dr Pearce evidently found inspiration within the Christian tradition for his life of prayer and meditation, but simultaneously he has come under other spiritual influences. This account of his spirituality and his initiation into healing brings out a problem for which I have no ready answer. How is the Church in fact to relate to and understand the whole range of alternative spiritualities that are on offer today? It could be fairly claimed that many of the people in church pews would rather not be faced with the demands of a spiritual discipline at all. If this is true then we are hardly in a strong position to attack and condemn those who sincerely practise spiritualities which are not necessarily pure Christian in their pedigree. The whole area is one where a considerable degree of discernment is necessary. Here we can only state that there is a problem of evaluation and assessment of these spiritualities from the Christian perspective, and not offer any simple answer.

Dr Pearce expressed to me the belief that everyone is a healer. The healing of Jesus was not in his eyes an aspect of his divinity but of his perfected humanity. As far as Dr Pearce was concerned the vocation for everyone to be a healer is implied in the words of Jesus when he said, 'Greater things than these shall ye do.' But in no sense is healing ever an automatic process. Not only does it require a spirituality of an appropriate kind on the part of the healer, but it also requires co-operation at the deepest level from the person seeking healing:

> It is my experience — take cancer for instance — that the fundamental need of people with cancer is to be enabled to pass through a process of personal transformation and, provided that the physical condition of the person has not passed beyond the point of no-return, that this will set free the springs of self-healing in the person which are the divine in action. Only when we recognize that, and start to be able to help people at the level at which the sickness has originated, in other words neutralize the causes within them, are we really going to be able to enable them to be healed. Healing and cure are not to be confused.

Later in our conversation I returned to the subject of self-healing being in some way equated with divine power. Dr Pearce clearly believed that the capacity in man for restoring himself to wholeness was the divine at work whether or not the individual recognized it as such. This is an unusual insight, but it indicates how far Dr Pearce has moved from seeing the body as some sort of machine. Rather he understands it as an organism shot through with the power of God moving it towards wholeness and health. The task of the healer and of the person seeking healing is to remove whatever might be preventing the divine and natural process of moving towards wholeness:

> I believe the force at work in healing is what we call God. I also believe that it has — I use 'it' deliberately, because I think we devalue God by creating him in our own image — also properties of intention and love which you don't find in just the ordinary inert force. Take the cell, the molecule, each sub-atomic particle, the force in it is the

Divine, the Divine creating. In that force we must recognize properties which are not commonly recognized in forces, of direction, intention and love.

Healing then is made possible by the field of one individual interacting with that of another in positive recreative fashion. He continued:

> If you reckon that the disordered field with which you are interacting has been disordered by a source at a different level from it, the psyche for instance, you must do something about that disturbing force. Otherwise, once the effect of your interaction has worn off, the force will produce its destructive effect. That is why so many spiritualistic healings do not stick. They are working at only a superficial level, sometimes called magnetic healing. The person keeps going back, and that is dangerous because in the end they become psychologically dependent on the healer. Whatever disturbance may be in the healer may be picked up.

Translating what Dr Pearce is saying into a Christian framework, the meaning is clear. Illness may have its origin deep in the roots of the personality, like some long-forgotten guilt or anger. Unless that cause is removed, no amount of tinkering with symptoms, whether through healing or drugs, is likely to bring lasting healing. Spiritual or inner healing is first necessary for the physical healing to take place.

Dr Pearce then went on to talk about some points made by the American psychologist Lawrence LeShan about the links between illness and inner motivation. LeShan in a talk given in 1983 had identified three reasons why people want to get healed of cancer:

> *First*, people want to get healed for the obvious reason that they don't like being ill. They don't like therapy, they don't like being faced with death. They have far too much living to do, unfinished business.
> *Secondly* that they may get well, may be healed for the sake of another person or to enable them to cope with a particular situation.
> *Thirdly*, that they want room to do their own thing, to find their own music, to sing their own song in life, to find their own means of expression.

The body, LeShan maintained, would not mobilize its powers of healing for the first reason. It would mobilize them to a limited degree for the second reason, to the extent that it may contain the disease long enough to cope with a particular situation, to see the family through college, or to nurse an ailing spouse to the end of his life and so on. But then when the emergency is over, then it switches off. Only for the third reason, that they find what is their own essential thing in life, will the healing take place. When they have found their own music, that which expresses them in life — that is, the process of transformation — can healing begin. It doesn't just apply to cancer, but applies across the board. I work with cancer because it is the way into people's thinking these days. It is the bogy disease of modern times; it epitomizes all that one is dealing with.

Again, it would not be difficult to translate the ideas of LeShan into Christian terminology. Just as we believe the nature of God to be creative love, so we also, if we are to live in his image, must express ourselves in love in the fullest sense, and become involved in some aspect of the work of creation. Such creative activity may take one of a multitude of forms, but it will be a true form of self-expression such as we find in our most treasured relationships. Both in our love and in our creative activity we find what we are really meant to be, and in Christian terms that means to discover what is the will of God for us. Dr Pearce's idea of the movement within us towards wholeness being the divine in action can also be taken a bit further. We are consciously to co-operate with that movement towards wholeness not only at a physical level but with every level of our being. In this way we can more closely live in accordance with the pattern for life that God has set before each one of us.

Dr Pearce further expounded his ideas on healing by describing to me exactly what took place at one of his healing/counselling sessions. The first task, as he saw it, was to enable the patient to know himself as he had never known himself before:

A cancer patient coming for the first time I would first of all need to convince that the body has its own way of dealing with cancer. That there is a power of self-healing even in cancer is something for which I lay out the evidence. I will then talk about the so-called cancer personality and the way it develops. Very often it is through a lack of childhood love or childhood appreciation, forcing people into a self-deprecatory situation where they have a poor self-image and a necessity to justify their own being. They fail to see that their value lies in themselves, and that no life is of greater value than any other life. From there we will go on to discover what is the trigger point, the reason for their cancer developing. This will involve a fairly detailed personal history, right back as far as they can remember, so that I really know all the things that have happened to them, how they relate to other people and so on. One has to teach them the importance of love, loving others and loving themselves. It is almost a cliché that you cannot be healed unless you love yourself — that means value yourself, not in a narcissistic sense. And that only by loving yourself can you express love to others. One has to teach them the truth of forgiveness, forgiveness of others and forgiveness of themselves; the truths of responsibility, that they are responsible for their deeds and actions and they will reap what they have sown. Equally, others have responsibility for their deeds and actions and they will reap what they have sown. Therefore any sense of resentment or retaliation is inappropriate and in fact destructive. One has to teach them the damaging effect of fear, to learn to take quite literally the counsel to take no thought for the morrow, for the things of tomorrow. They have to be taught to get a right sense of values for the things that are really important. I teach them the lesson of faith that all things are being taken care of if we can only see it. There is the difference between needs which will always be met and wants which will not necessarily be met. Finally there is the lesson of subjection and obedience. Do the thing that is in front of them without any self-doubt about it, knowing that none of us are tried beyond our capacity, but that the strength to meet the trial comes in the moment of trial and not before.

Dr Pearce commented that all that he was telling his patients was in the Sermon on the Mount. It was so important to arrive at a level of self-understanding because one could find that a lot of the heat and stress of a situation could be taken away for good. Without the burdens from the past the patients were so much freer to look to the future with a positive and open attitude, so that they could indeed be helped. Cancer patients were often in a fatalistic state of mind that everything was inevitably downhill for them.

I then asked Dr Pearce about the sensations that those who experienced laying on of hands reported:

They will sometimes say, 'nothing at all'. Sometimes they will talk of a sense of heat or vibration. Sometimes they will get up looking and feeling different people. Sometimes they will weep. I had someone the other day who thought she was fine, but was astonished to find in all this an enormous emotional release. It is important to get people to ask themselves the question, not, 'What have I done to deserve this?' but 'What has this been seen as, that I may learn from it?' In cancer one has found again and again that many patients, and certainly the survivors, will say: 'Thank God for this experience. This is the greatest thing that could ever have happened to me because I can see in myself the growth that has taken place. This is an experience that I would never otherwise have had the opportunity to undergo.'

Amid all the wisdom that I was able to learn from Dr Pearce about healing, there remained one or two blind spots. He was not able to give any positive evaluation to the existence of charismatic healing, assessing it as a dangerous form of hysterical manipulation. That had been his experience and he was unwilling to envisage that it might sometimes be used by people of great tact and insight. His method of healing also lacked the dimension of prayer during the counselling session. Prayer was something he kept till the moment when he judged that the obstructions to healing had been cleared. These are minor criticisms when we consider how far Dr Pearce has moved from being a conventional GP to embracing a new vision of the totality of man, as well as searching out a broad and compassionate method of healing. We should also be thankful for how much he personally has done to bring a new spirit into the care of cancer patients. We may hope that, for the sake of such people, this spirit will be adopted by more and more of the doctors and others responsible for their care.

We move on to our second doctor, whose story is very different from that of Dr Pearce. I shall call her Jean, though that is of course not her real name. Jean works in the Midlands as a part-time GP. She also practises homoeopathy. My conversation with her did not go into the detail of this side of her work, though clearly, as we shall see, the philosophy of homoeopathic medicine has affected her attitude to the medical model and enabled her to assimilate the possibility of Christian healing with little difficulty.

Jean described to me her early Christian background:

I have always been a Christian really. I say this in spite of the fact that I was not baptized until adulthood. I went to Sunday School, a Baptist one. It was war-time and we were evacuated and my father was away in the forces. In fact my mother said I was to have been baptized — it had all been arranged, but we were evacuated and so it had to be abandoned. It wasn't important to her in any real sense I suppose. But I went to a Methodist church as a youngster on my own — quite a lonely sort of church-goer as well. I was seeking very much but I never really found anything there. I went very regularly over a period of four or five years as a teenager and there weren't other young people there. So I don't know what I was going for, except seeking. At university I joined the Christian Union, and we went to St Martin-in-the-Fields to a rally. I was one of the people who went forward and accepted Christ then. I had that experience but it was a long time ago. Then I was married. My husband is not a Christian, but he has no opposition to my belonging to the Church and taking part in things. I got baptized when my children did. We didn't get them baptized as babies because of my husband not being a Christian, but they came to the sort of age when they asked about it. I read to them about it, and talked about it, and said, 'You can be baptized if you want to be.' They were quite excited and really wanted to be baptized. So we went and saw the Vicar and he talked about it to them. We had quite a session — a tea-party. So it was arranged for them to be baptized. And then I said: 'Oh, by the way, I haven't been baptized.' He said, 'Well, perhaps you'd better be.' My confirmation was very much an off-the-cuff thing. I talked about confirmation a few weeks after I had been baptized. Perhaps I should be confirmed now. And he said: 'OK, yes, I'll give you a few books.' A week or two later he rang me up and said: 'Would you like to be confirmed today? The Bishop is here and he is doing someone else.'

Jean's somewhat casual introduction to the Christian life had been supplemented by two experiences which most Christians have never had. The first was the discovery of Transcendental Meditation. This is one point of contact with the otherwise very different experiences of Dr Pearce. It was learnt before the events of her baptism and confirmation. She reflected on that first experience in this way:

I suppose in a way it did act as a means for my stopping, reflecting and getting myself into some sort of order inside. And I think it is a very good technique for people who are suffering from anxiety. It is very good for stilling the mind. I actually had a complete revulsion after I had gone a certain time and I had become a Christian properly.

In fact I abandoned it. But then I changed it, and instead of using the mantra I had always used before, I just used Jesus as my mantra. That worked very well. I still use the technique in a sense quite often but not on a regular basis. My life is not orderly enough to use it much. It was very much part of my opening up to more spiritual things. The Church has no means of offering anything like that to ordinary people who just want the technique.

The second experience took place after Jean and four others had set up a healing prayer-group in the parish where she was a member. The four asked the Bishop to come and talk to them about the gifts of the Spirit. At the first meeting the Bishop just talked, and then at a subsequent meeting he laid hands on them, and all four received baptism in the Holy Spirit, and spoke in tongues. She spoke about the experience with a certain diffidence, but it is obvious that the charismatic impulse has remained an important part of the group ethos, though it has never been dominant or obvious to those who come as visitors.

Jean then told me the story of her healing prayer-group. She had herself been the instigator because of a need in herself to pray for the sick more than the Church gave her opportunity to do:

We started our healing prayer-group as a meditative group, with the idea that I put forward: principally that there just wasn't enough praying going on for people who were sick locally. Our intercessions in church were much too brief and quickly passed by. I would go with a great burden of people to pray for, whom I couldn't necessarily name anyway because of the confidentiality of doctor and patient. I wouldn't have time to flick through half a dozen of them before it was all over, and we were on to the next bit of the service. So this was really my cry for help. This all took place six or seven years ago. We were very lucky in that we had a priest to start us off. He came and talked about it to me and B., who is a Vicar's widow and was very interested in the meditative approach. J. also came to the first meeting of the group and gave us a wonderful start. We met, there were twelve of us the first time. We've been meeting regularly twice a month ever since. He encouraged us to be a lay-led group, and to have a period of silence at the beginning of the meeting. This, to my sorrow, hasn't always been met with, because it depends so much on who is leading. Some of the groups have been very wordy and very pious — over-wordy, far too much.

The group over the years has had its ups and downs, but Jean's commitment to it, together with that of two or three others, has clearly provided a source of strength. This enabled it to survive and prosper even when the membership was changing fairly regularly. Jean mentioned that at times the numbers had increased to nearly thirty, but then just as they were ready to split up into two smaller groups the numbers had dropped again. Sometimes only three of them had gathered for prayer. Jean then spoke about the style of leadership which she adopted when it was her turn to lead, as this was fairly frequently because she was the organizer:

> We always sit in a circle. J. gave us reasons for this — so that there is no one at the head. Also so that we can all sit together in an equal group; we have the means of holding hands as well to strengthen our union. I've used quite a few different means of visualization with the group. Often my picture as we start is of our circle being filled with light. I sometimes talk about this light, because it is quite real to me, and it is very good because one does really feel it in the group once we've started. We dedicate our meeting just with the Lord's Prayer to start with; it may be more than that. We usually have a reading, usually a biblical reading but it depends on who is leading. Or if one of us has been reading something particularly appropriate then we will bring that along as well. We have a period of silence, reflection, meditation or whatever you like to call it — but the way I like to picture it now is simply sitting quietly and opening up to God. I have in the past gone through many times 'helping people to relax'. As a group they were very shuffly and ill-at-ease on being told to sit and say nothing and do nothing. Some of this came from relaxation, which I learnt a long time ago when I did a bit of psychiatry. It helps put people at ease actually to go through the process of helping them to let their muscles relax and sit comfortably. If you have got one person who is fidgeting and coughing and obviously not relaxed, it tends to distract the others. But nowadays it's really not necessary. And it is surprising how quickly, if you have got a few people like that in a group, the rest of them soon tune into a meditative mood. They will open up and relax, open up to God and to each other.

I then asked Jean about the encouragements the group had received from their task of praying for the sick in terms of people actually receiving healing. Her answer did not reveal striking miracles, but the group was rather sustained by a sense of the rightness of what was being done, and the way it fitted into a Christian ministry of love and compassion. But she told me that when the leader went round the circle inviting a prayer of thanks for any healings they knew about there was a lot to give thanks for:

> Certainly a number of the members of the group, those who have come regularly, have had healings themselves. I haven't documented it — it's an ongoing thing so I haven't singled out any one. One member of the group was badly troubled with arthritis, and was very distressed and disabled with it. She has witnessed to her own healing. She hasn't used any other sort of medicine, she hasn't done anything else different. But we have all prayed for her and she has hands laid on her in the group. Over the years we've had a number of people who've come just for a few times while they have a need for personal healing. They will often stay and talk afterwards as well so we know what they have come for. The group offers a talking-out support and this has become a function of the group.

Jean went on to describe the way the group was not confined to any one of the churches of the town. In practice, however, the core membership were all Anglican. One development of the group is a ladies' Wednesday group. This meets in the mornings in people's homes and is another caring prayer-group. She mentioned that the only man ever to have visited this morning group was the Roman Catholic priest, who had wanted to see that it was safe to let his flock attend it. Apparently he was satisfied. The Anglican clergy also have been involved from time to time:

> We had very much help from our Rector at the time. We talked it through with him and asked him if it was all right. He said, 'Yes, I am going to come along and see what it is like once you have started.' His wife became a very firm member, and our Team Vicar again is a pretty regular attender when time allows. Both he and the Rector thought it was a lovely peaceful time. They felt so relaxed because they knew they were not going to be asked to say the Grace or say a final prayer. They felt it was filling a gap, because there was no other service or function of the Church that was providing this sort of approach.

I questioned Jean as to whether the existence of the healing group had actually affected the ministry of the clergy more radically than just being an oasis of peace and prayer in the middle of the busy parish. One might have hoped that the ministry of healing would work its way into the day-to-day work of the clergy in their visiting. Her answer appeared to suggest a negative. If anything, her answer appeared to indicate that the clergy used the group to refer sick people to that they encountered. The group had not challenged them actually to do something directly themselves.

The main event in the history of the prayer-group was the advent of healing services. Jean and the other members of the group saw that they were not reaching directly many of the sick, because the latter were not prepared to enter into the informality and intimacy of the group. The healing service was a way of taking healing prayer to a far wider group of people:

> We had our first healing-service at St Luke's-tide, three years ago. It took place at St Chad's. And although it is a beautiful little church, it wasn't a good choice in terms of access. It was a one-off, just to see how it worked. Because there is no approved form of service, we made up our own. Well, we had that, and it was very successful. There were certain things that obviously we felt we could have done better or different, looking at it afterwards. But the fact was that it was well attended, about thirty to forty. And that was for a service that was out of the ordinary. We didn't have a blaze of publicity or anything. It was just quietly announced that there would be one. The Rector led it. There were a lot of lay-people assisting in one way or another. There were people reading and praying in the service. Two clergymen were present. I and one of the clergy formed one pair while another of the group joined with the other clergyman for the other pair at the laying on of hands. A lot of people came forward for the laying on of hands, which surprised the Rector who didn't think that there were going to be people coming forward. He hadn't had anything to do with the healing ministry before as a special thing. We were dragging him along but he wasn't in the least bit reluctant. He was just saying a bit, 'Where are you taking me?'

Jean went on to describe some of the personality crises that had from time to time affected the group. She also touched on a fascinating area, the link between mental illness and forms of religious enthusiasm:

> Sometimes it becomes difficult to disentangle the psychic/spiritual gifts from symptoms of illness. Last Saturday I had a phone-call from a friend who is a 'new' Christian. She was ringing about a small group not far from here. She told me, 'We have a young girl who has been

wonderfully blessed with the Holy Spirit and has received all the gifts.' Somehow my heart sank as she told me, because it sounded wrong just in the way she was talking about it. And as she went on it became obvious that the girl was having a schizophrenic breakdown, and was very seriously ill. What was even worse was that the husband was non-Christian and was frankly anti-Church. This was making him even more so. This can be a very destructive force, when something like this happens.

I then asked Jean about the part that healing played in her practice of medicine. She told me that she had been involved in healing first of all, long before she became part of the prayer-group, but at the time hadn't recognized it for what it was:

I went to visit a patient in his home, an old man who was dying. He was in a good deal of pain and distress. He was having injections of diamorphine but he was suffering dreadfully from nausea. It seemed to be related to the dose of diamorphine, which meant he had to have other drugs to help control it. They weren't working and he was very restless — he was pale, sweaty, he was moaning and tossing and turning the whole time — and it was one of those ghastly situations. His lovely little wife was doing her best to cope, but she was obviously very tired and very distressed. He couldn't even sip a cup of tea or anything. I went into his little bedroom, and there he was in this state. I put my hand on his arm and I was just stroking him a little bit and trying to communicate with him, but he was far too far gone in his pain even to respond to that. And I felt so hopeless and so sad that it should be like that so I just shut my eyes with my hand on him and prayed for him. I prayed for him to have peace. I sat there for a few minutes like that, and what stopped me from sitting there any longer was the fact that I got this pins and needles in my arm, sitting in this unnatural position. So I got up and walked over and talked to his wife for a few minutes — she was talking about the schedule and showing me the nurse's notes and so on, and asking me about a dressing for his legs. And we were turned away from him while we were at a table the other side of the room. Suddenly I became aware that he had stopped moaning and groaning, and we both turned round. I thought for a moment that he was dead. But he wasn't, he had gone to sleep. And he was breathing nice and peacefully. So I left after a little while. His wife said, 'That's good. That's the first sleep for a long time.' And when I went back the next day, she said: 'He's had a marvellous night's sleep. He slept from right when you came and he woke up this morning; he wasn't sick and he wasn't in pain. He wanted his cup of tea, which he enjoyed.' And he asked for the family to come and he was lucid and had a lovely last day. He died in his sleep the following night with no drugs. That was an obvious healing, but I didn't recognize it at the time. Then when I started reading about healing a few years later I remembered this incident. It was nine or ten years ago.

Jean told me that she prays with her patients whenever she feels it appropriate. She found it less easy to pray in the context of the surgery than in her own home. It was most natural when the patient was either in distress or in pain. No one had ever refused when she had asked if she could pray. She explained her practice:

> I have no embarrassment about prayer. There would be certain people that I would feel I could not say, 'Can I pray with you?' to. It is something that one does with a certain amount of sensitivity. But if you know your patient, or you know your feelings enough to know you can use prayer — sometimes I will pray out loud and sometimes I pray silently — then I will use prayer. Sometimes people like to know what you are praying for them. The prayer-group experience is important. You cannot do this prayer in isolation.

Jean went on to explain that she preferred to use a wordless prayer when praying for her patients, though obviously she recognized the need for words sometimes, whether with the individual or at public healing occasions like services:

> My prayer is a sort of visual thing, visual in the mind, of seeing whatever is wrong well and right again — of actually refashioning it like plastic or a speeded-up film. I hold it into God's light, because I visualize the healing power from God as being a golden light, which is why I mentioned before that our circle is filled with light. That particular energy of God, the power of the Holy Spirit, or however you want to word it, is what transforms the sick, the disease, the injured part back to health.

Jean mentioned finally that prayer formed part of her preparation for every surgery:

> I regard myself as a Christian, and before I start each surgery, I sit for a minute and pray, so that whatever work I am doing I am doing in Christ's name. I dedicate each day, and usually it is twice a day that I

actually praise and say 'Thank you', to Christ, 'because you are here, you are with me, and I can trust you.'

Holistic medical ideas lay at the basis of much of Jean's attitude to the practice of her profession. She criticized in a fairly radical way the old approach to the human individual as a complicated machine, and she wondered if the old respect given to the medical profession still held good. Her first statement on this subject was particularly startling:

> I don't think our medicines, particularly our modern medicines, have much to do with healing. I think they control symptoms, they help to alleviate people in distress. Giving drugs doesn't have much to do with the healing process. I am first and foremost conscious of trying to help someone when they come. They come because something has gone wrong in their lives in some way or other, and that distress may be at a deep level. They may need an awful lot of help and prayer and so on. They may have some physical symptoms that merit some medicine. They may have a peptic ulcer, and OK, yes, we might give them something that might help to heal the ulcer up quicker. They may have an infection and need an antibiotic, but that is not the prime thing they are complaining about — that is what they present but it is not what their illness is. Their illness is a much deeper thing than that. The mechanistic model is a means of helping people to get on with their lives while hopefully they are getting healed. I don't think people develop symptoms or diseases without there being a disturbance of their harmony. Their life is out of balance in some way. And it may be in a physical way, it may be in an emotional way; it may be due to all sorts of factors, and obviously in a ten-minute, five-minute consultation you can't have any idea of what is going on in their lives. But if you see someone a number of times, even with a short consultation, you begin to ask the sort of questions that find out if they have got imbalances that are obvious. I mean, if they are eating the wrong sort of diet, or if they are living the wrong sort of life-style, that is not conducive to health. Or perhaps they have got emotional problems, and these sort of things. Obviously as a doctor one would quite rightly explore all these sides with them. But often what you are doing in a surgery is just patching up the most superficial bit, you are filling in the crack with a bit of polyfilla and sending them off again.

Jean mentioned the difficulty she had had in arriving at these insights into patient care. She mentioned for example that the mechanistic model reigned supreme during her training. Her Professor of Anatomy at medical school, for example, had not allowed the use of the word 'mind'. There was no such thing as 'mind', it had to be 'brain'.

I then asked Jean how these insights into medicine fitted in with her relationships with the other doctors around. She answered with considerable frankness:

> I tend to see a slightly different section of the patients than they see. People tend to come to me because I listen, which they don't tend to want to do. And they think I am a bit of a fool because I sit there and listen to people, and spend more time with my patients than they do. I don't get paid any more, you see, for doing it.

I finally questioned Jean on how she saw the process of healing at work. In answering this she was clearly influenced not only by her Christian instincts, her homoeopathic training also lay behind her answer and the choice of language that she used:

> I think that the process of healing is associated with the restoration of balance of the whole person. I always picture illness as being a superficial manifestation of a disorder or imbalance in the whole system. It is what Hahnemann called 'the vital force' that is at the centre of that, that holds the system in balance. If your vital force is deranged, then you are ill. And I think that what happens in the healing process is that sometimes it is just too much out of balance for it to restore itself. We are made very well to heal spontaneously, but sometimes the forces are too great, and they are too long continued, so that that state of imbalance becomes locked or fixed. It requires some sort of energy to blow it back again. The energy is not something one can picture in a material or concrete way at all, but I think it is at a purely energy level. I think that the maintenance of health is something that requires energy anyway. This is where the power of healing comes in; it is something we are constantly suffused with. But at times when forces are against us, when you are poisoned or injured or under tremendous emotional strain (which is rather like a poisoning process), that balance is so badly out that it needs something more than just the gentle suffusion of healing energy to restore it. And so a shot of healing energy is needed.

Jean's free use of the language of alternative medicine may raise a problem for some of my readers, particularly those with medical qualifications. Once again it must be stressed that the experience of healing is such that in trying to describe it all our ordinary language concepts are stretched. It was thus tempting and indeed natural for Jean to use one conceptual framework which became available to her through her training, in this case in homoeopathy, and the broad themes of holistic medicine. Taken as a system, these ideas could no doubt be criticized either from a scientific or from a Christian point of view. But a readiness to criticize the words that she uses should not blind us to the fact that there is a real difficulty for her and for anyone else involved in the ministry of healing when it comes to talking about it. This whole study would perhaps be unnecessary if there were a generally-accepted vocabulary and framework of ideas for talking about the reality that we call Christian healing. It is precisely because of the lack of a widely-accepted language that the confusions and difficulties of communication abound. Jean's words have, I believe, to be read in this spirit, as an attempt to use words to describe the indescribable.

SIX

Itinerant Charismatic Healers

If there can be said to be divisions in the world of Christian healing, the most obvious one exists between those who call themselves Pentecostal or Charismatic and the rest. The way in which certain Christians operate in a world of miracles, signs and wonders is disturbing and even distasteful to many other Christians. In looking at the comments sometimes made by 'mainline' Christians, that charismatic healing is 'extreme' and 'dangerous', one detects a certain amount of incomprehension, rather than objective judgement. It is true that there are charismatic healers who operate in a most extraordinary way, and who suggest that to use doctors is to show a lack of faith (I have heard them). But it is wrong to suggest that every healer operating within a charismatic framework belongs to an irresponsible fringe. We may find their message disturbing or unpalatable, but we cannot dismiss or ignore them in any attempt to understand the whole phenomenon of Christian healing.

In choosing three men involved in the itinerant charismatic ministry I am aware of having exercised a certain degree of discrimination. Two of the three are individuals to whom I owe a great personal debt, and I cannot be sure that they are indeed typical of this group of healers. There are also others within this group with whom I suspect I might have considerably less in common. I have deliberately avoided healers who insist that theirs is the only correct way to practise this ministry and who shun contact with other Christian groups. It is for others to say whether by avoiding the intolerant fringe among Christian healers I am failing to do justice to this group as a whole. But I am, I feel, able to present the flavour of this rather strange world of itinerant charismatics, even if I have not necessarily chosen the most typical exponents of this expression of healing.

The story of my wife's healing has been told in chapter 1. I attended subsequent meetings of Peter Scothern on occasion, and found the services impressive for the sheer openness and integrity of Peter himself. I have a hyper-critical attitude to preachers whose task appears to be to initiate into jargon rather than to lead their hearers into an authentic experience of God. I also find myself disturbed by preachers who use fear as a means to coerce people into the Kingdom. Peter was guilty of neither of these failings, and thus I listened to him with pleasure and profit. I also knew, when the time came for me to arrange an interview with Peter for the purpose of this book, that he would understand and sympathize with all that I was trying to do. In this I was not disappointed. Never was he to suggest that the method he practised was the only way to mediate the healing power of God.

Peter Scothern in some ways appears to contradict all that the main-stream Church stands for in this country. He has no denominational base, and his authority is the authority that he has built up for himself over his thirty years of evangelism and healing ministry. In other words, he stands outside the structures of the organized Church. His ministry is to travel at home and abroad, preaching and conducting healing meetings in any centre that will welcome him. He was trained in a largely forgotten independent Pentecostal training college known as Lynton Bible School, founded by Principal D. G. Parker who was associated with the Pentecostal Jeffreys brothers of the 1920s. Peter Scothern's ordination and the title 'Reverend' were given him by this college even though the college had no official links with the Pentecostal churches. In other words his ministry was from the beginning independent in every way. Such an independence from church structures would have horrified me two or three years ago, but now my tolerance and capacity to recognize the activity of God in unlikely places has grown manifold.

Peter began by telling me his early history as a Christian. He had begun life as an Anglican, and then because of a move of house he stopped attending church for a couple of years. An illness and a deep sense of unworthiness led him into an experience of Christ at the age of about seventeen, and he became linked with a Methodist church. But although he had resolved his spiritual crisis he still had his illness. His account of what he did about this is worth recording in full:

> Now my immediate reaction after this was to resort to the Scriptures in faith for my physical need. I had no one to counsel me and assist me in my new spiritual life. I remember distinctly one evening speaking to the Lord in a very personal way, 'Lord, I need your help and counsel about this. Is there anything you have to say to me on this matter?' I have always conducted a very simple relationship with God through the Holy Scriptures. What invariably happens is that if I ask for help through the reading of the Scriptures there comes a divine response. It did on this occasion. I turned to the fifth chapter of James — almost coincidentally I turned there — and the first words that seemed to leap out of the Scriptures were 'Is any sick among you?' Of course that question was enough, because I then read on with great interest what followed. 'Let him call for the elders of the church and let them anoint him and the prayer of faith shall save the sick.' Well, to give another side of my simplicity of scriptural knowledge, I thought the 'elders' were of course the people of the church who were elderly in age rather than in spiritual experience. So I was rather disappointed when, in response to my request, two servants of the Lord came to see me, as one was in his younger years though one was elderly. They arrived and I pointed out the verse in James which I wanted them to act upon. The first question that arose was the question of the anointing oil. I hadn't given this any serious thought. So I proposed that they went down to the shed beside the house and brought along the oil and anointed me. As far as I was concerned oil was oil whether it was olive oil or whatever kind. So you can imagine my spiritual surprise when they came back into the bedroom with this can of oil — it was 'Three-in-One'! Immediately I saw the spiritual significance. They asked me how much oil they should anoint me with. I said 'Put plenty on,' and they put it on and it ran down my face. It was a question of obeying the Scripture thoroughly as far as I was concerned. Then they began to pray. But there didn't seem to be any element of faith in their prayers. So I stopped them, and said, 'Say the prayer of faith'. They said, 'What is the prayer of faith?' So I said, 'Pray that God is going to heal me, I have no doubt about this.' So they prayed a second time, rather more positively than the first. An amazing thing happened. I was charged with a spiritual power. One moment I could feel all those draining symptoms of my weakness — I suffered from nervous exhaustion with internal complications — then I was charged with this beautiful

power. I can't describe it. It is indescribable really. Immediately my weakness and all the discomfort and the pain that I was experiencing disappeared and I was alive. It was as if I had been plugged into an electric current; that was the most blessed experience, and for half an hour this experience was maintained. After half an hour I felt so strong, refreshed and rejuvenated that I got out of bed and dressed, though it was evening-time. I went downstairs, my appetite promptly returned, and I felt hungry for the first time in days. That was the turning point. Within three or four weeks medical folk were satisfied that there was nothing wrong, and I was back in business doing a full day's work, and that meant thirteen hours in those days. I knew something supernatural and wonderful had happened to me.

Peter then found himself invited to speak on the local Methodist Circuit about his experience of being healed. This brought him into touch with an elderly couple whose grandchild was terminally ill with some form of paralysis. They invited Peter to visit this child so that he could give the parents a word of encouragement. Neither Peter nor the grand-parents thought in terms of actually praying for the child's healing. Peter recalled visiting the child for the first time, and how touched he was by the sight of the little girl having to be helped to eat an ice-cream. The mother showed Peter a chart indicating the special diet that the child was on, but this was only completed for twelve weeks, the expected length of the child's life. On that occasion Peter simply told his personal story of healing, hoping that this would help in some way. But then, as he told me:

I returned home and that night I had a vivid dream. In this dream I was once again in the same little room with the same sick child. Then certain things happened which were to change my whole attitude to the divine healing ministry. We were alone. The little girl was lying there and I was suddenly conscious of the divine presence. I half looked round to the rear and there in the open door stood a figure and I had no doubt who it was, it was the Lord Jesus. No words passed between us but what did happen was this. I was conscious that the Lord came up to me and from behind me guided me to the child. Then he took hold of my hands and laid them on the little girl. And then I looked up, because I was so amazed by what had happened, but the divine presence was no longer there. But there was a sensation in my hands which compared with the experience I had had when I

93

was healed. It wasn't through my whole being but particular to my hands. And as I laid my hands on this child it was as if my hands were glued to her person with this power. After a little while the power ceased and I became natural again. I removed my hands from the child but the child was full of life. And I saw that she had experienced what I had experienced when I was personally healed. Without hesitation she jumps off the sofa and begins playing with her toys. Incidentally in the final stages of the dream I was weeping for joy, and when I woke up I was weeping naturally. And I lay awake for some thirty minutes meditating on it.

The next stage in the story took place on the following day, when Peter discovered that the grandparents of the girl had had a similar dream, and were waiting for him when he returned home from work. They immediately all set out for the child's home and found the child's parents out and the child in charge of a baby-sitter. Peter, left alone with the girl, did exactly as his dream had commanded him:

I laid my hands on her in the name of the Lord. And as I did so the same blessed experience that I had had when I was personally healed occurred. The power of the Lord came upon me and the little child was blessed. Now the only difference was that there was no immediate response in the little girl; she didn't immediately jump off the sofa and begin playing with her toys. There were still signs and symptoms of her illness. I suppose that under normal circumstances I would have been grossly disappointed, but I wasn't. Somehow deep down inside me I felt that all that had happened up to this point was so remarkable and divinely ordained that my faith wasn't shaken because there was no immediate miraculous response. Over a period of a month her wholeness returned, her paralysis disappeared. The first I knew about it was that I got a telephone call down at the office one morning to say that the little girl was now going back to school. It was now the end of term and the only exam she was able to take was her writing exam, and in this she came out top of the class.

This event was to change Peter's life, as he found himself in demand as a circuit speaker and called out to minister to individuals in their homes. He tried to continue both his career and an evangelistic healing ministry, but eventually was forced to choose to make the latter his life's work. This was in 1950. He then went to Bible College, choosing Lynton College for its association with the Jeffreys brothers. These brothers, founders of the Elim Pentecostal Church, had conducted an itinerant healing ministry in the 1920s and 1930s. From there he entered a full-time itinerant evangelistic and healing ministry. In the early days he depended entirely on invitations to speak and minister at various churches around the country. These would be for periods up to three weeks. In 1953-4 he was invited to conduct a series of meetings in the United States, and he recalls a particular incident in the opera house in Philadelphia which was to lead to a lasting association with West Africa. While alone in the vast building, which seats five thousand people, preparing for his evening meeting, he was suddenly aware that he was not alone. He assumed that a cleaner had come in, but instead of responding to his question, the figure, dressed in white, began to prophesy. The prophecy was that he was to respond to an invitation to preach in West Africa which would be awaiting him when he returned home. The figure then disappeared into the background:

> I jumped up and started going round the platform area to find out who it was. There was no one there. Even then it did not dawn upon me that it could be a supernatural visitor. So I went to prayer again. And then I was conscious of this presence a second time. The instructions were repeated, and I knew then that this could well be a supernatural visitor. At this point I had an anointing of God which was absolutely phenomenal. When I tried to stand up to go near to this being again I found I hadn't got any legs. I had to fall to my knees again and I was in awe and wonder a second time. I was like that for well over an hour. Eventually I found I could stand, and I went to the door and found it locked.

Peter explained that, according to the electrician who had let him in, no one could have entered the building while he was on his own.

The letter that the angelic visitor had spoken of was waiting for him in England on his return, and this led him to spend a period in Nigeria conducting evangelistic crusades. He spoke briefly about enormous gatherings of up to twenty-five thousand people. The story of these got back to England, so that from then on he was in greater demand to lead crusades in this country. It was at this point that he set up the organization 'Voice of Deliverance', to handle administration on his behalf. There was a good deal of correspondence to be coped with, along with the circulation of newsletters and latterly a tape ministry. The West Africa connection has continued up to the present, and Peter frequently spoke on other occasions of the wonderful things that God had done in Sierra Leone in 1984.

An early problem which Peter had to face was that of denominational allegiance. From the early days a variety of denominations had used him and his healing and evangelistic gifts. At one point a particular denomination had tried to persuade him to join their ranks, but he was glad now that he had resisted that attempt, because it had become clear to him that he could be of help to all the denominations if he was not identified with any one in particular. He clearly valued his role as an itinerant, even though it was not readily understood by the denominational churches. The itinerant, he explained, was the one in the New Testament who was both a pioneer of the gospel and who also had a role exhorting and encouraging newly-founded congregations. Over the years his ministry had sometimes been more concerned with the long term support and encouragement of a particular area, and at other times he had maintained a far more wide-ranging evangelistic ministry over many centres. One particular place with which he had once had a long-term association was Hainault in Essex. Peter had gone to that congregation over a period to support Trevor Dearing in his ministry. Another particular focus of his ministry at this same time was in West Wales. Peter recalled speaking to congregations of twelve hundred in Lampeter, and sometimes there were hundreds more waiting to get in. Peter felt that the large crowds at this stage of his ministry were part of the overall phenomenon of charismatic revival which was at that time burgeoning in places all over the country. He spoke of the dramatic healings that had taken place in Lampeter. A blind girl was given her sight back, and one Matty Evans was dramatically healed of a throat cancer. The media had apparently taken a great interest in the meetings.

Apart from the five-year period when most of Peter's time was spent in Hainault and West Wales, his main ministry has been one of going on a monthly basis to a variety of centres to conduct healing and evangelistic services in halls. His aim is to reach people who have little contact with the churches. He recognized that ideally there should be preparation for these services and follow-up afterwards. But given the impossibility of talking to a large number individually, there is still the possibility for God to reach people and bless them even in a limited way. The occurrence of a healing miracle at one of his services also can set off a chain of reaction, with, as he put it, 'tremendous spiritual repercussions for the glory of God and the Kingdom of God'. Peter recalled how at a meeting in Lincolnshire, on the Monday before we met, two or three people were miraculously healed. At the meeting there was a group of Christians who had come out of sheer curiosity. But their curiosity was changed into intense questioning and wonder as they sought Peter's help in coming to some understanding of what had taken place.

I asked Peter about the exercise of his healing ministry, and what he found to be important in maintaining it. He replied that at every stage he had studied the Bible for what it had to say about healing. This study of the testimony of Scripture, combined with the experience of actually doing it, had matured into an established gift of healing:

> The ministry evolves directly out of my personal relationship with the Lord, of that I am absolutely certain. I find that in respect of my relationship with the Lord and my ministry of healing I must keep a very humble and open mind. Looking at the ministry of Jesus I am amazed when he makes the statement 'the works that I do are not my works but the works of my Father,' and 'I speak not my words but the words of my Father.' His total reliance on the Father is one of the mysteries of his life, and yet I feel I must identify with it.

The important thing for Peter was never to allow his experience to override the possibility that God had something new to teach him. As he put it, 'There is a balance between years of experience and knowledge and the need to keep a humble and open spirit before the Lord. You're learning every moment of the day something new in this ministry.'

Peter went on to talk about the insight that he was given into the needs of the individuals who came to him for ministry. He said that quite often he is faced by a number of people at a public meeting who come for laying on of hands, but that he is checked by the Holy Spirit from laying hands on one particular person:

Then you know you have got to question the person first. For example, last evening I was about to lay hands on this person and I just couldn't. So what I do then, if I get this check by the Holy Spirit, is to talk to them, open a conversation, and I often find this will illuminate the reason why. And it did. I saw very clearly that this person did not have a proper relationship with God and had just come to the service because of having seen it advertised. I questioned him about his relationship with the Lord, and this led to a spiritual discussion which was beneficial to the person.

I thereupon put the question to Peter how far a person's healing depended on his relationship with God. He then told me about a business man who came to one of his services without any Christian background, but who was miraculously healed. Six weeks later, when he decided that his healing was permanent, he decided he must go to church at least once to give thanks for his cure. He went to the local Baptist Church, and was converted and became a Christian:

> This is the exception rather than the rule. The Lord, because he is omniscient and knows the future, knows how a person will react if he healed them first, and counted on their making a spiritual response at a later stage as in the case of this man I mentioned.

Healing and a renewed experience of God went very closely together, though Peter told one story of a woman who was healed, but never made any personal commitment of her own. But her testimony succeeded in bringing many others to Christian commitment. In other cases where individuals were healed with no apparent Christian convictions, Peter saw that, 'In the long term it was linked with the overall pattern and mind of God to bring salvation to his people.' In other words, for Peter every case of healing had some spiritual purpose and meaning, whether or not the individual concerned became a Christian. This discussion led naturally into the problem of the individual who failed to receive healing at one of his services, and Peter's answer to this question again came back to the individual and his relationship with God. The attitude of faith was important, and he believed that many who failed to receive healing did not deep down expect anything to happen anyway. But that was not all:

> If a person comes to one of my services for healing and doesn't receive

healing, there's a reason — I state this very frequently — or reasons, and the next step is to find out the reasons. Suppose you went to a doctor, and the doctor checked you over and wrote out a prescription, and said you've got so-and-so wrong with you. If after you'd dosed yourself for a couple of weeks and you were no better, you'd go back to him. He would give you another check over, and try something else. I think we should adopt this same attitude to divine healing, and contact the minister to whom we had been led, to go and say, 'Look, nothing has happened.'

Peter told me that he welcomed letters from people who had failed to receive help at one of his services, and he normally sent them a twenty-point questionnaire which covered many aspects of their lives, including their relationship with God and Christ. He would then help them to search out the reasons, through sending them books and tapes in the first place, or, if they requested, by personal interview before one of his meetings:

In other words, we like to try to get to the bottom of the problem of why they are not healed. This is a far more positive way of dealing with it than throwing everything to the wind and saying, 'This doesn't work'. If you did that with your doctor, your doctor would finish with you overnight.

It was clear that for Peter and for all the others described in this book who practise a healing ministry, healing is seldom an easy option. It requires hard work in many cases, and a degree of self-examination that many people are unwilling to give. To expect an instant miracle, without any readiness to change in any way, is perhaps to trivialize the ministry of healing, and certainly not recognize in it the activity of God.

I questioned Peter about his experiences when administering the laying on of hands. He admitted that there were sometimes distinct movements and vibrations in his hands, similar to the vibration that he had had when he himself was originally healed. But there was no pattern to it:

Sometimes I have a remarkable experience, and the experience is like a warm breeze flowing over me and over the sick people. They've told me this. It is as if someone has opened the door and let in a beautiful warm balmy air or wind, and often when that happens people are just overwhelmed and just sink to the floor — it happened last night. Last night I began praying for the sick and I felt nothing. I got to about the third person and this beautiful breeze came over me, as if the Lord had drawn near and was breathing on me. The dear man in front of me just collapsed on the ground. I hadn't even touched him. I just walked up to him and the next minute he just crumbled and was overwhelmed. He said, 'Some kind of glory just overwhelmed me.' When I lifted him up — he had an arthritic condition of the spine — we got him to bend down and jump up and down on the floor. There was a stiffness there for a little while, but at the end of this process he was amazed at what had happened to him, and he had been in this condition for a long time.

I asked Peter whether he had noticed certain situations where a miracle was more likely to happen to an individual. He had often made the point that miracles, instantaneous healings, were the exception rather than the rule. Far more common were healings of a gradual nature, and this was in fact the experience of Frances my wife. He answered that there was no discernible pattern. The continually unexpected nature of the healing power of God always surprised him. Sometimes the people who were healed miraculously were expecting a miracle, sometimes not. 'To put it in a nutshell, I maintain my relationship with the Lord with an open heart, a humble spirit, ready for God to do anything at any moment, and the wonder of this ministry is that you never know what is going to come next.'

He gave me a final example of the way the Holy Spirit had prompted him to do something unexpected. A Methodist lay-preacher had asked him if he could do anything for a neighbour of his who had cancer. Peter said that he could have offered a general prayer, but instead, prompted by the Holy Spirit, he took a handkerchief and prayed over it:

> We laid our hands on that handkerchief and he took it immediately from that service at 10.30 to the sick lady. He went to visit her and laid hands on her with the handkerchief in his hands. I had given him instructions to do that. By midnight there was a tremendous difference, a marked difference. On the Monday after the Saturday she was due to go for exploratory tests for a serious operation. And when they did the tests they could find no trace of the cancer. It had completely disappeared in that short period of time. I have a wonderful letter of testimony here.

Before we leave Peter Scothern and his ministry, we should dwell for a moment on an issue which I would have expected to have formed an insuperable barrier between us — the barrier of fundamentalism in biblical interpretation. Most evangelists of Peter's tradition take a conservative view on questions of biblical interpretation, and Peter is no exception in this. Quite often in general conversation he would quote a passage from Scripture and make a point of teaching on it. I must admit that I did not always find myself able to agree with the way he had used the passage. He was able, for example, along with all conservative interpreters, to find parallels between Old and New Testaments in most unlikely places. He would also give great prominence to obscure passages of genealogy in Genesis. Peter early on accepted that I could not go along with all these methods of biblical exegesis. But I was not in any sense written off because I failed to fit into this overall conservative view of the Bible. On my side, I can accommodate Peter's views in many areas because I see that his theology is not derived from an arid intellectual fundamentalism, a bibliolatry, but is at every point qualified and indeed informed by an active and genuine encounter with the living power of the Holy Spirit. As Peter said early in the interview, his resources for healing are partly based on his experience and partly on his searching of Scripture for guidance. As an Anglican with sympathy for the charismatic dimension of spirituality, I can accept that Scripture is or should be interpreted through our openness to the Holy Spirit. In other words, Peter's fundamentalism is subordinate to his living experience of God, and thus it never plumbs the depths of aridity or sheer intellectual confusion of the 'dry' Conservative Evangelical. Apart from its qualification by his deep spirituality, Peter's fundamentalism is also tempered by his genuine humility. As with many healing evangelists, Peter does not possess any of the suffocating arrogance of some evangelical preachers. He sees each person who comes before him as a child of God who may have something to teach him whatever his experience. Humility is perhaps one of the key qualities of genuine Christian healers, as they never cease to give thanks for the power of God at work in their lives. Humility in one area of life spills over into the whole of life and protects its bearer from the arrogance, aggression and intolerance that many of us associate with a certain kind of fundamentalist believer.

There is an element of irony in the fact that of all the people I talked with for the purpose of this book, the one with whom I have the least in common from the point of view of religious background is the one who in fact initiated Frances and myself into the actual experience of healing. This chapter must then contain an account of the events that led to this, as well as describing the man and his background.

In April of 1983, before this book was conceived or thought of, the local paper in Hereford contained an account of a visit to the area by an American healing-evangelist called Jim Sepulveda. This was a few months after Frances's original experience at the Shirehall with Peter Scothern, so we knew enough to regret that we had missed the meetings where Jim Sepulveda spoke. But then, through various contacts around Hereford, stories of the meetings began to reach us. One story was of a group of secondary-school children who had witnessed healings in their lunch hour, causing considerable consternation among the school staff. A leg was lengthened, eye disorders corrected, and children went home praising God, to the bemusement of some parents and the irritation of others. Our curiosity was aroused, and we looked forward to the return of this remarkable person, Jim Sepulveda, to our part of the world.

The autumn of 1983 saw the return of Jim Sepulveda together with two other evangelists, and the three of them were booked to speak at various centres in South Wales. Jim was not due to speak in Hereford on this occasion, so Frances and I travelled to Mountain Ash, in the heart of the Welsh valleys, to hear him. This meeting happened at around the time when the first tentative plans for this book were taking place. So I set out for Mountain Ash having a sense that the meeting was to be the beginning of a chapter in my life. It was in fact a beginning in more ways than I could possibly have imagined at the time. When we arrived we were shown into a fairly typical Nonconformist Welsh chapel. We sat at one side so as to be able to see what was going on at every stage. We had arrived late, but Jim had still not made an appearance, and the local minister was leading the congregation, which was not large, in choruses. Eventually Jim arrived and began speaking. He is a small well-built man of Spanish/Mexican extraction, and his personality soon communicated itself to the audience as one of great gentleness and love. What he said was surprisingly simple, but as with Peter Scothern it had tremendous warmth and power. The appeal to the congregation was not to commit themselves to a fundamentalist or Calvinist gospel of salvation, but simply to become aware of the power and love of God in their lives. Then the mood of the service shifted, so that the power and love of God became not just talked about but enacted and experienced. When Jim talked about feeling the glory of God there in the service, there was indeed a dramatic change of atmosphere which was palpable. The congregation were then welcomed to come up and be prayed for and one by one they came up, a trifle unwillingly at first. Each one spoke with Jim and then was prayed for. Most collapsed at his feet, and Frances when she was prayed for described this sensation as being filled with electricity. In her case, as with many others, Jim did not lay his hands on her head but merely touched her on the shoulder. At one point a man who had not come up on his own was called to the front, but Jim stopped him some twenty feet away from the podium. He was then prayed for, and he proceeded to fall down even though no hands were near him. I puzzled then and since over the nature of the power that seemed around everywhere that evening. It seemed that though there was an emotional atmosphere in the chapel, the power was independent of it. Jim's personality was of such transparency that through him a spiritual power and love seemed to pour out to fill the rest of the chapel like light filling darkness. Jim was acting as a kind of catalyst for a spiritual power from beyond. The word I used to describe the power that night was 'tangible', and it was quite unlike anything we had ever experienced before. I certainly felt that there was nothing false or contrived about the falling-over phenomenon, 'slaying in the spirit', as it is sometimes called, even though I would be hard pressed to explain exactly what was happening.

Our encounter with Jim might have gone no further than as members of one of his congregations, but for a series of coincidences which made it possible for me, together with

Frances, to interview Jim and Don Martin, another healing-evangelist, in May 1984. This took place in Alsager while the two of them were on yet another tour of this country. We and they were under pressure of time, and in some ways the interviews were less than satisfactory. Don gave us a clear exposition of the context of the healing ministry as he understood it. He stressed how he believed that the Holy Spirit was indicating to him that the old structural denominational forms of church life were giving way to new spirit-filled groups which belonged to no-one beyond themselves except Christ. He felt that denominational forms of Christianity were man-made, and were obstructing the free flow of the power of the Holy Spirit. He even described them as being under the thrall of principalities and powers. I record these rather un-ecumenical comments because they represent a point of view widely held by charismatic groups and house-churches. There is in them a certain understandable logic at work. If your experience of Christianity is one of having access to power and glory every time you pray, then you are going to be dismissive of older forms of Christianity which both lack that glory and also appear to you to have rather cumbersome structures of authority. If your local community has access to the Spirit of Truth, then why do you need others somewhere else to tell you what truth is. Don was too much caught up in his conviction of his thesis for me to be able to challenge it effectively. Part of me wanted to concede that he had a valid insight which the denominational churches might do well to hear, the other part of me said that this was hopelessly naive, and could not work in practice.

Don's conversion experience was by British standards extraordinary. Brought up with virtually no knowledge of the Christian faith, he received Christ through watching an evangelistic television show. He then received healing over the telephone, and almost at once began a healing evangelistic ministry. Hearing such a testimony makes one question whether the sheer simplicity of it has not something to teach us. If conversion and faith can happen within such a short space of time, a conversion manifestly blessed with spiritual gifts, one wonders whether the traditional churches have not made everything very complicated. If I had not actually met Don, and heard him speak at a Full Gospel Business Men's Dinner, I would have found all kinds of reasons for believing his conversion and healing ministry to be somewhat trivial. But whatever else it was, and I am sure that it can be criticized on various grounds, it was in no way trivial. The same Holy Spirit at work in the rest of the church was working through Don, and in a powerful way. That Holy Spirit had found a way into his life and ministry having bypassed many of the routes that I used to think were an essential part of the journey.

The interview with Jim consisted of much biblical quotation and anecdotal material about his healing ministry. Much of this was lost when the tape recorder refused to function for the first two thirds of his account, which he spoke at an incredible speed. Jim, unlike Don, had had some kind of nominal Christian past, and so he was prepared to be more generous to the main denominations. Like Don's his story of becoming a Christian was, to put it mildly, unusual. He was suffering from chronic heart disease at the age of thirty-five. Something drew him to an evangelistic meeting at a sports stadium, and much to his astonishment he was called up to the front by name by the evangelist. He tried to escape out of the stadium, but then a voice said to him, 'What have you got to lose?' Having received a blessing, he found himself falling over. The next stage of the story took place when he came up for heart catheterization, which was carried out in spite of his improvement after his experiences at the stadium. While he was being catheterized he suffered a massive heart attack, and was given up as dead for fifteen minutes. When he came round he found a cloth over his face, and the surgeons were over on the far side of the room getting ready to leave. So convinced had they been that he had died, that they had not bothered to sew up his wounds. During his 'death' he met a figure he identified as Christ, who told him that he wanted him to return to earth because he had many things he wanted him to do. Christ told him, 'Be obedient to me so that I can show myself through you.' Two years after this, during which time he had acted as an usher for the healing-evangelist who had first helped him, he was invited to speak himself. He suddenly felt an overwhelming need to call out a particular woman at the back for prayer. The woman eventually came up and immediately fell over and received healing. The next thing he knew was that there was a queue forming in front of him. Now he saw himself as simply being used by God to help and inspire groups and congregations of whatever tradition with the gifts God had given him. He had no particular Pentecostal emphasis in his teaching, though clearly his whole personal spirituality and sheer presence was charismatic in the fullest sense. In the things that he said, and from some remarks of Don's, it appeared that the most extraordinary physical manifestations of light and fire actually happened to him personally. For example, Jim told me, and Don had mentioned it as well, that he, Jim, had glowed physically with a kind of fire for a whole night. I mentioned this to someone well experienced in meditation, and they confirmed that a similar experience had happened to them when in deep meditation. Jim talked about this and other events, not in order to impress, but in a kind of slightly puzzled way that such things should happen to him which were clearly examples of God's power. No one who has met Jim could have any doubts about his humility. The theme of light also came up when I asked him about calling people up at his meetings. He told me that he saw a light on them, and knew from experience that the Holy Spirit wanted to minister to them. He also indicated that on occasion he could see through people with a kind of X-ray vision when it was important for him to know something about that person's physical condition.

During this interview I was blowing hot and cold, as I wondered whether I could communicate the things that were being told to me without losing the sympathy of my eventual readers. I recognized that there existed enormous cultural and theological barriers between us, and I was not able to establish the fairly natural and easy communication that had been and was to be a feature of all my other interviews. The whole of this part of the chapter might well have sunk and never surfaced again but for what happened at the very end of the interview with Jim, and this was to change me and my wife. In view of this I have included some account of Jim and Don, even if I am handling material which was so extraordinary that it might have been tidier and easier to have left it out.

During lunch Jim questioned Frances about her illness, and Frances replied that though the arthritis had gone there still remained a certain amount of residual damage in the joints which with God's help was disappearing. He then went silent and little more was heard from him during the meal. After lunch, time had been reserved for our talk with Jim, and he referred to this piece of conversation again. He told us, 'God has told me that I am to pray for those joints before you go.' At the end of the interview he proceeded to pray for Frances, and once again I sensed that tangible aura of power in the room which I had experienced in Mountain Ash. I quickly moved over to Frances to be ready to catch her in case she fell, and I arrived only just in time. I was more certain than ever that my awareness was not responding to any emotionally charged atmosphere. There simply was no time for emotions to become charged, as the whole incident had taken only a few seconds. When Frances eventually got to her feet, she spoke to Jim about a friend of hers called Juliet, who was that day having surgery in a London hospital. This friend had been born with congenitally deformed hips, and now at thirty-one was having the first one reconstructed surgically. Frances had been to see this friend during the previous fortnight, on her very first solo trip to London since her illness. Jim stood looking at Frances in silence with great intensity for a moment, and then told her that she was to go to Juliet and lay her hands on her hip and pray for her healing. After telling her this, Jim laid his hands on her shoulder and he told her how he could see what he called the anointing of the Spirit upon her.

We left Jim, Don and our Alsager hosts and set off for home. Frances was feeling somewhat light-headed after this experience, and we didn't quite know how to react. It was agreed that we should go to Juliet to do as Jim had instructed, but we made no real plans as to how we should carry it out. The following week, by coincidence, was the summer half-term, and so it was easy for all of us to go to London via Reading, the home of Frances's mother. At Juliet's bed-side we were suddenly faced with the need to put into practice the instruction Jim had given. Frances turned to me and asked if I would pray while she laid her hands on the hip. With a strange sense of confidence we saw that Jim's instructions were followed. As we left the ward after bidding our farewells to Juliet, Frances told me that the bones of the hip had moved under her hands while we prayed, even though they were under traction. My immediate comment was, 'This is where the hard work begins.' If we were to be agents of healing in some way, then we were both in the future going to have to work hard to be worthy of such a privilege.

For the next four weeks Juliet was to be in traction, and we knew that no further news was possible from her end. We had the expectation of a miracle but no means of confirming it. Eventually the letter we had awaited arrived, and Juliet informed us that the hip that had been operated on gave her no pain, and immediately after coming off traction she had succeeded in lifting her leg up at right angles, to the astonishment of her doctors. Their reaction was to speed her down to the operating theatre to do the other hip. The promised wait of ten to eighteen months between operations had now contracted to five weeks. Juliet is still recovering from the operation as I write these words — the second operation was not so speedy in its result — but she too is convinced that she has witnessed a miracle. Her problem has been to find anyone in her family or friends with whom she can share it. We are looking forward to the time when she will come and stay with us, when we can learn more about the way that this event has changed her as well, and deepened her understanding of God.

Frances and I have been decisively changed by the event of Juliet's healing. It has changed my attitude not only to my research, but also to my whole ministry. Just as it seemed spontaneously right for Frances and me to act together in the case of Juliet, so we have felt drawn to continue to pray for and lay hands on the sick as a pair. This activity has grown and developed over the past year as we gain experience and encouragement from our actual praying with people.

In the space of a year we have prayed with a number of people. In no sense have we felt moved to make this a public ministry, and we would be unwilling to suggest that the particular ministry we have is an appropriate one for everyone who is sick. There is an inbuilt tension between wanting to pray with every sick person in the locality and an awareness that only a minority will be open to receive what we seek to mediate. Christian healing, as we have seen, is no soft option, but makes demands on the individual. There are many who are not prepared to take on the package.

What we have done is simply to wait for people to arrive to seek help. Some have come to us through our prayer-group, some from a Christian doctor, and one from a neighbouring clergyman. In two or three cases only have I taken the direct initiative myself, and suggested to an individual that they seek the laying on of hands. For the time being, at any rate, this is the pattern that we adopt. It is not yet a completely 'confident' ministry, even though God has been able to use it in a quite remarkable way. Meanwhile we remain ready to follow in any direction that the Spirit may seek to take us in the future.

At the beginning we used to combine the laying on of hands with the administration of the sacrament of Holy Communion. Now we would only do this if the person concerned were confined to bed. The regular practice is for us to invite the sick person to come to us, and spend quite a lot of time talking out every aspect of their situation. We show them that we are not doing something to them, but through prayer they are being drawn up into a process, into the orbit of God's love and healing power. That process needs their co-operation and indeed effort if it is to be effective in them. I find that the natural language to use to describe this 'orbit' of God's healing power is the 'Kingdom'. When we open ourselves up to God by a process of repentance and acceptance of his will in our lives, then he can accomplish his will in us, and that includes his will for our wholeness. In the process of opening up to God, there is often an exposure of guilt, fear or past hurts. These, once revealed, form part of the prayer that is offered for healing.

Another way in which we describe the healing process is to talk about going to the 'place of healing'. This language helps to emphasize once again that nothing is being 'done' to the sick, but that they are being drawn into a process, a process that is always there, but only made effective when we shed obstacles that we have built around ourselves. The place of healing is where God's perfect will can be accomplished, and this will is concerned not just with our physical condition but also with our lack of wholeness in every area. We tell people as they leave, especially when prayer has evidently begun a process of healing, that they must now try and live within this orbit of God's will all the time. They must expect God to act in their lives, and try and see in the day-to-day events of life that God is indeed active. The healing process, of which they are a part, is just one small indication of the truth that God is indeed living and active in his world.

We have been fortunate that none of the people we have prayed with have latched on to any absurd or unrealistic ideas about the ministry of healing. Indeed their understanding of its significance has surprised and humbled us. On one occasion we suggested that a lady should go to a meeting of Peter Scothern for a further laying on of hands. She put us in our place by telling us that surely the laying on of hands that she had received from us was the vehicle of God's healing and she didn't need anything further. Another lady with a chronic lung condition had a set-back at which I expressed some regret. She said, 'Oh no, this set-back was caused by my getting 'flu. For the past eight years I have gone into hospital with pneumonia after 'flu, but this time, though I was worse, I was still able to stay at home. That is because of the laying on of hands.' Her quiet confidence in the healing power of God is an encouragement to us as we move slowly into this area of ministry to which God seems to be pointing us.

The remarkable thing is that with every individual who comes to us we learn something new. Every one who has come to us has presented a different set of underlying problems. It is as though we are being built up in our experience gradually, so that we are prepared for the future. Sometimes we feel we are led to the problem by some form of inspiration. As long as we bring the whole interview under God, then he is able to use it to teach us something new and use it for healing at many levels. Somehow those who have come to us have nearly all accepted the vision of healing and its demands on us that we present. The prayer that we offer is indeed a unified prayer of openness and trust which unites the three of us. We have seen something happen on almost every occasion. A young woman with asthma described a sensation of bands being broken from her chest and a swab of cotton wool being removed from her throat during prayer. A young lad of twenty with ulcerative colitis has improved so much after five months that he is off steroid treatment, and the distressing symptoms of the illness have vanished. What is still more encouraging is the new transformed attitude that he has developed in his response to his healing. He has not yet found any formal faith, but he is caught up in something which he knows is extremely important and which is helping him to grow as a person. Prayer seems to release in a person a new capacity for growth in the widest sense. We are still feeling our way forward, thankful for the guidance that we are given and the wisdom we discover as we actually do the work. There is a sense in both of us that we are learning as we have the capacity to absorb; God in some way is always a little ahead of us, leading us on further in our discovering of his will for healing.

On almost every occasion the people we pray with will volunteer what they have experienced during prayer. They all mention an all-enveloping peace, and some of them have mentioned that they feel strong vibrations coming from Frances's hands. Once we prayed with a woman whose relationship with her mother was strained. During prayer she saw herself reaching across the gulf between them to touch her mother. Frances was also given an image; it was of a woman sitting in a chair winding wool into a ball with the figure of Christ sitting opposite her holding the wool as she wound it. Before the woman left, Frances asked if her mother did a lot of knitting. 'That's all she ever does,' she exclaimed. These images often come to Frances during prayer. On another occasion, when praying for the young woman with asthma, Frances saw Christ sitting on the settee nearby. He was smiling and gently tossing the Ventolin tube from one hand to another as if to say, 'You don't need this any more.' The pictures are given, she feels, for the encouragement of the individual for whom we are praying. Certainly they do have that effect, and contribute to the whole healing process of which we are all witnesses.

Behind the work of praying with individuals, Frances and I have begun a small prayer-group. We meet once a week in term-time during the day. At this group Frances and I share with the others what we are doing and ask for their prayerful support. We also pray for individuals near and far who are sick in any way. Part of this time is giving to sharing insights that we have been given about healing, perhaps from the Bible or from something that has been said to us. I personally have found that the past twelve months have been a time of almost continuous personal and spiritual growth. Many times when I open the Bible new meanings crowd into otherwise rather dull passages. The experience of healing is very much an experience of the Spirit — it seems to transform and enlighten everything else.

Jim Sepulveda returned to Hereford and the surrounding area in the autumn of 1984. Frances succeeded in spending a couple of hours with him, and she came away greatly encouraged and helped. Jim had stressed the importance of obedience to God, and that when we are obedient to him he is able to lead us into the truth that he wants us to have. The healing ministry is one where there is learning all the time. There must be openness and humility at every stage. There was little that one individual could teach another about the ministry of healing, as it had to spring out of a relationship between them and God.

I suppose it would be true to conclude this part of the book by saying that what began as a piece of research has been taken over by something entirely different. The research has become something no longer apart from me, but belonging to my personality at the deepest level. I have moved from finding out about healing from the experts to discovering subjectively what it is inside me. What was begun as a book has become for Frances and me a way of life.

SEVEN

The Spirituality of Healing

In the course of my interviews I often pondered on the fact that healing has only comparatively recently been widely recognized in the life of the churches. I asked myself what, from a historical point of view, is around in the churches today that was absent, say, in the Victorian period. There is no evidence that faith is any stronger in the churches now than it was a hundred years ago. It is true that though theological trends were not favourable to healing in the very materialistic Victorian age, a theological antipathy is still very much with us, as we shall see in our concluding chapter. The reason for the widespread revival of healing seems to lie in a new spiritual climate that this age has discovered and made its own.

This chapter is an attempt to consider the spiritual context of the contemporary healing ministry, drawing both from the people we have interviewed and from a wider survey of current trends. But before we attempt to pin formal spiritual labels on the people presented in this book, I need to begin my observations on spirituality with a very personal impression arising out of my interviews. When I began the task of contacting people to speak to, I had no idea that I would be welcomed so warmly and given so much help so quickly. It is not every day that one meets someone for the very first time and is given so much intimate information about their spiritual and personal lives. I expected a rather more formal contact on the first occasion, with a need to go back again to put further questions and deepen the level of the discussion. This in fact was never needed, and all the interviews recorded in this book are based upon a single encounter in each case. I returned in one case only, to clarify points of detail. This openness on the part of those I spoke to about healing I put down to a great generosity on their part, and it did not occur to me until much later that this same openness was part of their qualification to be involved in a healing ministry. It was later still, after I had written the first draft of this chapter, that I suddenly saw what this characteristic of openness really was. The healer needs what I came to call a capacity for spiritual intimacy, the ability to get very close to the person they are trying to help in and through their life of prayer. In talking to those involved in the healing ministry, I was allowed to experience the same intimacy and generosity that they were used to giving to those who came to them for healing. Just as their ministry of healing developed in them a spiritual intimacy, so their ordinary dealings with others in any context displayed this quality.

As I reflected on the implications and characteristics of spiritual intimacy I came to realize that this quality of spirituality was not something we find in the traditional text-books on prayer. And yet spiritual intimacy is very much part of our contemporary scene, particularly within the charismatic movement. And it is of course not limited to this. Wherever there is informal prayer with an individual or in a group there is the possibility of closeness with that person or that group. The impersonal quality of so much that passes for Christian community, both now and in the past, has perhaps been a factor in the failure of healing to be widespread or acceptable. For many people there are deep problems to be overcome before they are able to accept the fact that love of our neighbour is about overcoming barriers to intimacy rather than just doing our duty to them. When Christians have discovered how to be open and intimate with one another as the result of their experience of God's love to them, then individuals discover a tremendous vitality and relevance to the Christian faith, and healing can begin to take place at many levels. Where worship is stuffy and relationships are formal and correct, or worse still, condescending or authoritarian, then it is easy to see how healing is inhibited and hard to realize.

Alongside the capacity for spiritual intimacy in the sense I have spoken of, I noted the great humility of all my interviewees. Humility is not only the human quality of not putting oneself forward, it is also a spiritual quality. It is a readiness to see the life of prayer as a preparation for allowing God to accomplish his will through the one who prays. Such an attitude is well summed up in the old precept, 'Let go, let God.' The spiritualities of those I spoke to were all concerned with this fundamental letting-go, whether it was expressed in the prayer of meditation or the prayer of charismatic release. I began to see how closely these two patterns of prayer were connected. The difference between the two was as much one of style and culture, as one of fundamental divergence. A common experience of being used in the healing ministry would I am sure act as an indissoluble bond between all my interviewees, whatever their styles of prayer. The quality of spiritual humility that united them (though this is not true of everyone involved in Christian healing) is to be placed alongside the spiritual intimacy I have spoken about. The two together form two important identifying marks of the authentic minister of Christian healing.

So far, what has been said has referred to my personal observations about the spirituality of a ministry of healing. I wish now to go on from my subjective impressions to look at the comments of others who have in different ways tried to make sense of healing, and of the spiritual demands it makes on those who practise it. In my reading on the subject I have only discovered two authors who have made a reasonably convincing attempt to look at healing in a scientific way: the American psychologist Lawrence LeShan and the medical researcher Herbert Benson. LeShan concentrates his study from the point of view of the healer and the spiritual qualities needed in him. Benson starts from the other end, and looks at the 'faith factor' on the part of the person seeking healing. LeShan has already been mentioned in the chapter on the healing doctors, in connection with his work of psychotherapy with cancer patients. His total output of published work shows him to be a man of the broadest interests, with the subjects tackled including holistic medicine, meditation and the implications of post-Einsteinian physics for our modern world-view. His understanding of healing is not, in my view, complete, nor does he write as a Christian, but his findings are so striking that they are worthy of our interest and study.

LeShan's main concern in his book, *The Clairvoyant Reality*, which was first published in 1974, is with the scientific study of the paranormal. He observes that with many paranormal phenomena the person experiencing them shifts out of normal everyday consciousness into a different dimension, which he calls the 'clairvoyant reality'. Here the paranormal becomes normal. He takes this observation into the whole realm of healing, having made a special study of some notable healers, including Agnes Sanford, Harry Edwards and Olga Worrall. Largely ignoring their interpretation of the healing process, he concentrates on what they actually experienced and did. In his analysis of the healings that he studied, he was led to divide them into two broad categories. In the first, 'Type Two', the healer was conscious of something happening in his hands when healing. The activity of healing was in some way an imparting of energy from one person to another. The nature of the energy he thought to be a kind of para-electricity; the healer is able somehow to concentrate his energy to help restore what has been lost in the sick or injured person. Dr Pearce's words provide us with a commentary on LeShan's Type Two healing. We may recall just one of Dr Pearce's observations about the dangers of this kind of healing: because it is operating at a low level of spiritual reality, there is the need for much repetition, and this may in turn lead to an unhealthy dependence by the patient on the healer.

The more interesting kind of healing which LeShan describes is what he calls 'Type One' healing. In this the healer goes into an altered state of consciousness, into a mystical state, the realm where all things are One. This state of consciousness is reached through meditation. In it the healer and his patient in some way become aware of a new relationship with the universe, or, to quote LeShan when talking about the patient, 'he was completely enfolded and included in the cosmos, with his "being", his "uniqueness", his "individuality" enhanced.' Such an experience creates a new orientation to reality which enables a movement towards wholeness and healing to take place in the one who experiences it. For LeShan, Type One healing enables the body by this new openness to the cosmos to fulfil its self-healing potentiality in a speeded-up or enhanced fashion.

LeShan followed up his analysis of healing by training himself to meditate in such a way as to be able to accomplish healing himself. He succeeded to his satisfaction in reproducing the phenomena of Type One healing, also training many of his students to do the same. But in his attempt to analyse and describe all forms of psychic healing, he recognized that there was a category of healing that he had not taken account of. This was the miracle, the instantaneous healing. He called this 'Type Five' healing. To achieve this the healer had to penetrate what LeShan described as the 'transpsychic reality', while the Type One healer was penetrating only the 'clairvoyant reality'. I record this extra dimension of healing although I feel that LeShan is here, from the Christian point of view, at his weakest. The contrast between these two realities is made against the background of a belief in an apparently impersonal power at work in the healing process. There is no notion of the grace of God or the Holy Spirit at work. If one takes the Christian insight, and belief in a personal God who may have some initiative in the whole healing event, then one is rather wary of an analysis that makes the process too tidy. LeShan is no doubt right to see spiritual preparation as part of the healing process, but the Christian would expect the miracle to depend partly at least on the inscrutable character of God's will, rather than on a particular form of human meditation, however highly developed.

My reason for quoting LeShan in this book is not in any way just to criticize him. LeShan's main observation, about the shifting of consciousness in order to enter the clairvoyant reality before one can heal, is of great interest. Although it is language that is barely recognizable to Christians, what he is talking about, when translated into Christian language, is simply spirituality. All healers, whatever their beliefs, are able in some way to open up to something beyond by moving outside everyday consciousness. Dr Pearce spoke about 'a peg of dissociation'. By that he meant something, a thought, an image or a sound, that would help the mind to go outside itself, to be no longer wrapped up in its own concerns but free to gaze on a higher reality. Words like 'contemplation' and 'meditation' are all something to do with what LeShan means by 'entering the clairvoyant reality'. The strangeness of his language should not hide from us the fact that he is making a valuable contribution to the understanding of healing. He is stressing the need for an appropriate spirituality if healing is to be effective. The fact that the spirituality he learnt for himself is not particularly Christian is for the moment not important. What is important is that every healer with an effective ministry, that he studied, had a spirituality, however broadly we understand that word. LeShan offers no grounds for believing that there are any short cuts for a would-be healer. We have of course to make some considerable adjustment in order to translate LeShan's language of altered states of consciousness into the theological language of prayer which is the way that our Christian healers speak. But prayer is in fact for each of them a shift out of everyday consciousness in some sense or another. In this way LeShan does provide us with a point of reference for considering the spirituality of healing from the healer's point of view, even though his conceptual framework is far from being a Christian one.

LeShan's account of the healing process passes quickly over another important part of the process of healing. The attitude of the patient towards what is done for him is obviously of crucial importance. We have seen some of the psychotherapeutic ways in which an individual is prepared for healing, and we have noted that the right attitude of openness is vitally important. It is here that our other writer, Herbert Benson, has something of interest to say from the scientific/medical point of view. He has worked on 'biofeedback', a mental technique by which certain physiological functions can be controlled. He has also stressed the importance of relaxation for health, and the need to escape from negative thought patterns. In his latest book, *Beyond the Relaxation Response*, Benson stresses the importance of belief in the whole process of getting well. Part of a doctor's task in helping a patient to get well is to encourage him to affirm his belief system, to bring into action a healing response within the body. Benson claims that the important thing is not the content of the belief or faith, but the focusing of the mind in this particular way, that produces an important effect for healing. He links this 'faith factor', as he calls it, to the placebo effect which medicine has known for a long time but, Benson claims, has seldom taken seriously. In his book, he records some studies he made in India, looking at the physiological changes experienced by Tibetan Buddhist monks while meditating. For him these studies strengthened his belief in the extraordinary power of the mind to effect healing. LeShan and Benson both help to put healing in a much wider context, and we can see how our studies are linked to researches made by individuals with very different perspectives and presuppositions on healing.

We shall return to a consideration of charismatic spirituality later in this chapter, but meanwhile it is important to consider the style of spirituality represented by Gibson Pattison, Gordon, and to some extent by Dr Pearce. Each of these three represents a tradition of Christian meditation that is not afraid to take on board ideas and insights from a broader religious tradition than Christianity narrowly defined. It is an observable fact that many of the creative spiritual writers of the last twenty years, notably William Johnston, Thomas Merton and Bede Griffiths, have introduced us to the idea that it is important to take into our spiritual tradition a concept of God which owes something to Buddhist and Hindu ideas. Monks the world over in every religious tradition have discovered many points of contact in their basic religious quest. We are not here witnessing a sell-out of Christianity to other world religions; rather our tradition is being greatly enriched simply by being exposed to the enormous breadth of spiritual experience known to men of other spiritual paths. If meditation is a valid spiritual exercise for Christians, then it would indeed be difficult to find a method for such meditation which owed nothing to the other main religious traditions. Christians have taken the techniques and made them their own, but they share with religious people everywhere certain basic beliefs as to the purpose of this work. Meditation is a method of inducing stillness, so that the ego, the centre of consciousness, can be transcended. The inner self is then released to 'know' and be joined to God or whatever name is given to the Reality beyond. There is a common understanding in all expressions of meditation that one needs to discover the 'heart', the non-intellectual intuitive centre of the personality, if one is to embark on the religious movement towards God. This language fits in well with the main stream of Orthodox spirituality, with its 'prayer of the heart'. To deny this whole realm of experience totally is perhaps to reaffirm the modern Western bias towards the intellect and reason. The fact that other, non-Christian, religions often seem to concentrate on the 'doing' of religion rather than on the 'believing' intellectual side, has made them attractive to many young people who reject what they see to be a concentration on rational assent in traditional Christianity. Gibson, Gordon and Dr Pearce all in different ways move within this style of Christian meditative prayer. Each of them would affirm the great power and effectiveness of this kind of prayer, not only for healing but also for their own personal relationship with God.

This broad tradition of meditative prayer is then one of the two strands of contemporary spirituality that appear to be at the basis of an effective healing ministry. In all my research on healing I failed to find anyone who was not working somewhere within this broad category or within the charismatic tradition. There are, as we shall see, important points of convergence in these two traditions. Some of those whom I met operated from both these spiritualities. The fact that both styles of prayer are widely practised today may also be responsible for the fact that healing is developing widely in a way that was seldom seen in the past, apart from isolated gifted individuals.

This presentation of healing as belonging to certain particular spiritual disciplines has a further consequence. This is the fact that it may be wrong and misleading to present healing as something as easy as saying the words of the Lord's Prayer. There is a cost involved which requires the would-be healer to reform his attitudes and inner life in accordance with certain principles of spiritual discipline. One idea for which I have found no evidence at all is that some objective sacramental act in itself is efficacious, independently of the would-be healer or patient and their state of readiness. In other words, God does not appear to bypass our prayer and intercession to effect a healing because of a sacramental rite being used correctly. When a sacramental anointing is performed, there is need in the healer for the same spiritual discipline and openness to God as there is in a layperson who just lays on hands outside a sacramental context.

I also see no evidence for the idea that the grace of orders gives a priest a special short cut to a healing ministry. Clearly though, in so far as the priest or minister is a true focus of the prayers of his congregation, then we should expect to see healings take place. But that is, as we shall see, different from an ordinary man's possessing an individual healing charisma or gift simply by virtue of his ordination. Such a charisma may be his from the beginning of his ministry, or he may find his way towards it through prayer and seeking it from God. The sacramental ministry of parish priests with the specific intention of healing is widely available, but it is my belief that such a ministry is chiefly effective when it is performed at the centre of a praying congregation. Sacramental Unction may also be a powerful means of ministration when it evokes in the person who receives it a response of openness and faith which in itself releases the healing power of God. But the normal pattern for an effective healing ministry is where an individual, lay or cleric, has a recognized gift for healing, or where a whole congregation takes seriously Christ's promise given to the Church that healing is a normal part of the proclamation of the gospel. We shall have more to say about this below, and about the place of healing services. The use of the sacramental means of healing also performs the important task of indicating to both healer and patient that the power is one that comes from beyond. LeShan was expressing this, in his own language, when he talked about healing as realizing that the patient not only existed in the ordinary mode of existence but also 'existed to the furthest reaches of space and time'. By bringing his patients into this dimension, the healing work is accomplished because they are brought into a new relationship with it, the Cosmic One. In the same way, the priest is able to demonstrate that healing is a process which involves a co-operation with divine power, and not something out of his own strength. But it must be repeated that the power of the sacrament operates in and through the focusing of the prayers of the congregation, or through the priest's special charisma, with its own spiritual formation and discipline involving intimacy and humility. All this is brought into the process of healing, and this is needed in addition to the readiness and preparedness of the one who comes for ministry.

Before we draw further general conclusions from the ministries of healing which have been examined in the preceding chapters, I should like to look at a further writer whose grasp of the spirituality underlying a healing ministry is probably unparalleled in this country. This writer is the well-known priest-doctor Martin Israel, whose works on the whole healing phenomenon are widely regarded and consulted. Amid all his writings there is one short article which I have found especially useful in my attempt to clarify what are the essential characteristics of a spirituality that undergirds a healing ministry.

The article in question is found in the volume of essays on the charismatic movement edited by David Martin and Peter Mullen called *Strange Gifts?* In this article, 'The Spirit of Truth', Martin Israel succeeds in finding a way of talking about charismatic phenomena which is both coherent and satisfying. For him the charismatic experience is 'an opening of the personality to the warmth of a universal relationship, so that a person who was previously shut up in himself, emotionally inhibited and unable to pray with real conviction because of stultifying intellectual agnosticism or personal pride, is now released to show himself to the world, even as a child.' This language of 'opening the personality' to the Holy Spirit and the simultaneous relinquishing of one's fears and insecurities, enables Martin Israel to be very positive about the whole experience, as being a 'full spiritual awakening' and involving a 'dynamic response to God's love'. Yet he is able to criticize the movement when it becomes exclusive in its attitude to truth, and 'tends to brush aside, if not totally ignore, any other approach to truth.' An emphasis on emotional and intuitional aspects of the personality has also a tendency to put reason to one side, and 'other aspects of truth . . . are then either ignored or else assailed as the work of dark, demonic forces that govern the material world.'

Martin Israel also explains why things sometimes go wrong, when he talks about the charismatic experience as bringing the believer 'face to face with the truth of the less acceptable elements of his own unconscious.' There has to be a process of love co-operating with discernment working 'together toward the healing of all that was aberrant and maladjusted'; otherwise these less edifying forces from within the subconscious can take over or become dominant. This opening-up process also may awaken intuitional and psychic processes which may have been buried by the conscious mind. Healing is just one of the 'fairly common expressions of spiritual release of the personality'. In other words, healing, for Martin Israel, is something that is latent in the personality but may be awakened by the opening-up process implicit in the charismatic experience. In so far as meditation has as its aim the same opening up of the personality, we are right to see the two spiritualities as very closely related. In both there is a transcending of the ego, in both there is the notion of release and opening up of the personality. For this reason it would be wrong to present one as being superior to the other. Personality traits may have something to do with the particular expression of spirituality that an individual finds accessible. Would it be wrong to see the difference between the two spiritualities in cultural rather than in theological terms? Certainly both appear, as far as healing is concerned, to be able on occasion to unlock the power of God to heal.

I questioned many people about the links between a charismatic spirituality and a meditational spirituality. One person gave me a fascinating insight about how she saw the connection working out. The charismatic was for her an opening up to God and the use of power in a broadly masculine or active way. The meditational approach to God was a feminine or passive opening up to that same power. I valued that observation because it immediately gave one a further insight as to why the charismatic approach to healing sometimes goes badly wrong. The knowledge of possessing the power of healing could become the ground of aggressive coercion towards those who came for ministry. A strong intolerant streak, which often goes with an unredeemed charismatic spirituality, combined with a masculine-type coercive awareness of power, is a recipe for disaster and total confusion. Disasters like this do occur on occasion among charismatic healers, and are all too often quoted as evidence against the whole group. I do not accept that such a judgement is either fair or rational. Each charismatic healer must be evaluated on his merits, and we must not prejudge any particular healer before we have looked at what he is doing. These potential dangers of a charismatic spirituality need to be set alongside the problems encountered by those who seek God through the way of Christian meditation. Here the temptation is to slide off into spiritualism or neo-oriental cults such as Theosophy.

In this discussion of power being used in an active or passive manner, we are entering a difficult area where it is sometimes difficult to distinguish between psychic or natural power and divine power. We have to accept the fact that there are many gifted individuals around who possess great powers of healing but for whom the idea of God is alien. They may be able to simulate many of the spiritual gifts, including speaking in tongues and possessing what in a Christian context would be seen as great spiritual discernment. Sometimes it is clear that we are dealing with natural or psychic gifts, while in another context it is evident that the gift is a divinely-given charism. Sometimes it is impossible to distinguish between the two. Gordon recalled the time when he felt that his group had healed a lady by the simple use of psychic power engendered by the group.

There are various possible answers to this problem. One is to say that the two, psychic and divine power, are totally different in kind, and that the one has to be condemned and exorcised out of the Christian. Another approach is to say that psychic and spiritual or divine power are two aspects of the same thing. The divine uses the natural endowments latent in the personality for its own purposes, and when the personality is purified then nothing can go wrong. But when the personality is corrupted by power-seeking or some other imperfection, then what begins as a divine spiritual power is quickly corrupted or at least compromised. At the one extreme we find the totally corrupted person using psychic power for selfish and evil ends. At the other end we have the person purified by prayer using another aspect of the same power for God-given ends. In the middle we find many others using power for a mixture of motives and ends, the good often being compromised by spiritual blindness or bigotry. All the spiritual immaturities to which charismatics sometimes fall prey can cause havoc with the way in which their spiritual gifts are exercised.

The typical Christian, viewing the world of charismatic gifts from the outside, might feel complacent when he sees the confusions and disasters that not infrequently befall the charismatic communities and congregations. But such complacency is out of place. The non-charismatic Christian is almost certainly guilty of the same spiritual faults, but for him they are hidden in his 'private' religion instead of being opened up by the charismatic release. Thus they are never revealed to scrutiny from outside. In support of the individuals and groups who are caught up in the charismatic spiritual process — and this of course applies to anyone who has found their way into a dynamic spiritual encounter with God — one must say that they are involved in a process of spiritual growth unknown to those who have never allowed themselves to be opened up by the Spirit of God. Just as spiritual gifts are opened up for them, so regrettably the human attitudes of pride and arrogance seem sometimes to flourish simultaneously.

Among all the varieties of healing explored in this book, a little more needs to be said about the approach of Roy Lawrence. He claimed strongly that in his case the gift of healing was something given to the congregation and not to the individual. Roy denied being in any formal sense a charismatic, while Neil Cosslett recognized this as part of his spiritual make-up.

Earlier in this chapter I spoke of the opening-up of individuals to the discovery of deeper levels of personality and gifts through the charismatic experience or the act of meditation. It would appear that such a process of opening up can take place not only for an individual but also for a group. Christ himself recognized the importance of true corporate prayer, when he spoke about two agreeing about anything on earth, finding their requests granted. What Roy Lawrence seems to have discovered is how to develop a congregational spirituality of sufficient depth and intimacy that the healing power of God can flow through. It was to this that I was referring when I wrote above about the priest's sacramental healing needing to be the focus of a praying congregation.

Gordon refers, in a different context, to the way that the group exercised an intense level of psychic power when thinking about the injured member of their group. Roy's people appear to have achieved, not psychic energy, but an environment and focus of concern where healing prayer is effective and powerful. Individually probably none of them could have done anything, but together something happened as the spiritual resources of the whole group were welded together. It seems to be true that the prayer of agreement, which we would call the prayer of intimacy, effects something, and this is quite different from lots of people simply praying for the same thing at the same time.

One can only speculate on the role of George Bennett in Roy's life. George appears to have infected Roy not so much with a charisma of healing itself, but of enabling a congregation to find its way to the 'agreement' and the degree of mutual intimacy and attentiveness to God which can make them an effective agent of healing. He has taken his charisma of enabling around the country, and by his preaching and evangelistic activity he has brought the message of healing to many centres and congregations. Roy indicates beyond any doubt that the ordinary congregation can exercise a ministry of this kind, but it does appear to require a very special prayerful environment, which may need to be built up over a period of time. The leadership will need to do much more than simply start healing services. There is a danger that these may become an end in themselves, an optional extra added to the weekly round of services. In this situation they can too easily become a static activity, rather than part of a whole process of growth into the special environment where healing in the widest sense becomes possible and effective.

Many churches round the country have healing services, and one is forced to query whether they are indeed leading their clergy and congregations into a healing ministry. A parish with healing services should not avoid the fairly rigorous self-assessment that is part of real growth into a healing ministry. Roy's vision for whole parish involvement is possible, but some parishes may be going through the outward signs and not achieving the inner reality. As long as this is sometimes the case, as I believe it to be, the most effective healing ministries will seem to belong to those who practise healing out of an overtly charismatic or meditational milieu.

Some of those who practise an individual healing ministry in this country are clerical. Perhaps a larger number are lay people. The fact that this book contains the accounts of more clergy than laity is a comment on the networks available to the author in his search for suitable people to interview. In a situation where the whole congregation feels called to a healing ministry, then it is likely that the clergyman, whether or not assisted by his leading laity, will probably wish to be the visible focus of the healing ministry in his congregation. In another situation a lay person may arise who in fact possesses an individual gift of healing. I hope that such people may be recognized and allowed to exercise a ministry even if the clergyman in charge may as a result feel threatened. The New Testament gives us no warrant for suggesting that lay people will not arise with such distinctive gifts. Healing, after all, is one of the many charismata given to the Church, and a priest should not feel aggrieved that this particular gift has not been given to him.

The Epistle of James, I feel, gives us some good advice about the conduct of a healing ministry in the context of a Christian congregation. When we study the passage about the calling of the elders of the Church to pray for and anoint the sick, it would appear that the whole thing really only makes sense when the congregation, or at least some of them, have already committed themselves to healing prayer and intercession. This is to repeat a point that I made earlier in the chapter. To offer the sacrament of anointing to a sick person where there is no commitment to prayer for the sick among the people is like celebrating Communion in a parish where there is no commitment to some kind of corporate life. The two, the sacrament and the common prayerful commitment to the intention of the sacrament, are inextricably bound up together. The minister, if he is to perform a laying on of hands or anointing, needs others to help him, whether by their presence or by their prayer. A long-term commitment to that kind of support makes far more sense than a sudden flurry of activity when a particular anointing occurs.

A final area needs to be discussed before this chapter is brought to an end. This is the area of exorcism. I have become aware during the final stages of writing this book how much one 'school' of Christian healing is able to perceive the demonic in many cases that come to its attention. I seem to have avoided coming into personal contact with this approach, and thus this position is not presented. I have however read, in *Understanding Alternative Medicine* by Roy Livesey, the statement that, 'What we need to recognize is that cancer is from Satan.' Immediately after this the author goes on to state that 'Some of these cancer treatments are from Satan too.' He is one of a number of modern authors who seem to want to put all healing into the realm of what we might call exorcism, though they would probably talk in terms of 'deliverance'.

127

Of all the people I talked to, only Joan spoke of her involvement with the power of evil as a factor in her healing ministry. Readers will have noted that, for her, evil was a force that entered into the human condition through a deliberate act of invitation. This interpretation of the force of evil in human experience is one that I can accept myself. Playing with Ouija boards and joining in Satan-worship is dangerous, and may cause havoc with the psyche. But to suggest that demonic powers are involved in human sickness, and are then lurking around ready to trap the sick when they look innocently to seek help from alternative health practitioners, is surely moving towards the absurd. I do not believe that Satan has any entry to the human soul except by deliberate invitation. This might be through deliberate involvement with the occult, or a conscious decision to promote evil, as through calculated hatred. As I have stated elsewhere in this book, I also do not believe that the use of natural healing powers is an example of Satan counterfeiting the powers of God and using them to entice the unwary into his control. It is merely a lower and less complete form of healing, unless it is dedicated to God and becomes, through that dedication, the means whereby the Kingdom can break through into the world.

The doctrine of creation tells me that God created everything and saw that it was good. He created the sexual side of man knowing that it would and could be used for evil ends and even for occult purposes. He also knew that it could be used for the highest form of human love and sharing. He created healing powers in human beings, and again he ordained that they could be used to his glory or could be a means for some to seek power and control over other people. Just because we do not yet understand these healing powers does not make them automatically become occult and Satanic. A conscious involvement with spirits in offering healing is of course dangerous and occult, but my impression is that the majority of 'natural' healers are not consciously mediums of any kind. There is a great deal about human beings that we do not understand. Under the new model of science, which we shall be exploring in the next chapter, we may quite soon come to understand such powers as being purely natural. The talk of energies and meridians may be just nonsense, or it may be a way of describing something real beyond our present scientific models. A frequent recourse to explanations involving demons and Satan leads me to believe that a Christian healer may himself have fallen into a trap. In his anxiety to protect his model of Christian truth, he is tempted to use unfair weapons. The effect of much talking about demonic powers may often be to terrify sick people out of their wits and make them ready to accept anything the Christian healer puts into their minds. We thus find here the type of healer which many people associate with the charismatic: the manipulative, 'infallible' and coercive type who risks bringing the whole group into disrepute. The question, I believe, to ask about any Christian healer is, 'Are they humble?' Without humility they run the danger of allowing the human dominating side of their personalities to be more obvious than the healing power of God. St Augustine said in a wise moment: 'Pride lies in wait for good deeds, to destroy them.'

I need to repeat quite clearly my own position after my study of the subject and my own experience of praying with the sick with my wife. Evil, by which I would mean a personal malevolence, does exist, and it is a factor to be reckoned with in the healing process. But I would strongly disagree with writers who see the demonic in everything they do not understand. As I say elsewhere in this book, some people equate whatever is inexplicable in terms of nineteenth-century science with the occult and Satan-inspired: for them, only what is explicable in terms of scientific proof can be accepted.

However, in the case of a Christian healing, I would accept that there is likely to have been an element of exorcism which may not be apparent either to the minister or the one who has come for prayer. Illness and disease have very often a context in the evil and disorder of the world, whether caused by the sin of the one who comes for prayer or by evil that comes from outside in some way. The prayer for healing may or may not contain explicit reference to the casting out of evil, but trust in the healing power of God and his readiness to enter the situation will often effect just such an exorcism, particularly after some act of confession. The practice of a ministry of healing is in some sense spiritual warfare, and to see it as less than that is perhaps to underestimate its nature.

My wife and I in praying for the sick now prepare ourselves by praying for protection from whatever evil may be involved in the person's illness. This is not based on some kind of superstition, but on a deep sense of the reality of evil in the world, and the need for constant vigilance. We would be unwilling to become involved in a formal exorcism, given our total inexperience in such an undertaking. But this aspect or dimension of healing is never far from our minds and our prayers when we pray with the sick, even if they show none of the signs of possession. I would here follow the wisdom of a group of exorcists in the Anglican tradition which suggests that possession is extremely rare, and does not arise from anything as relatively trivial as going to a homoeopathic doctor. But to lead a sick person out of the miasma of guilt or sin, whether their own or belonging to someone else, that has caused them to suffer at a deep level, requires a certain authority and confidence in the power of God over all that could oppose his will. This would appear to be a kind of exorcism, even if only God knows what exactly is having to be removed from the person's life to effect healing.

The reflections and observations in this chapter are offered as a way of starting the reader thinking about the whole topic of the spirituality underlying a healing ministry. These observations are just that, and are not based on scholarly research in the area of contemporary spirituality. But my observation is that there are new dynamic traditions of spirituality emerging which co-exist with the rediscovery of Christian healing in the modern world. If healing is indeed a breaking through of the Kingdom of God with love, forgiveness and restoration in its train, then we should be ready to examine with attention the spiritualities through which this is being discovered. The new spiritualities we have described are challenging us, in the same way that healing challenges many theological and institutional aspects of the Church's life. Healing involves all who become involved with it in a radical reappraisal of their spiritual priorities, as well as of their understanding of the way the Church exists and operates in the world today.

EIGHT

The Context of Christian Healing

Alongside the rediscovery of Christian healing, there is a quiet but growing revolution in human thought which is beginning to make the idea of healing much more acceptable to numbers of people both in and out of the churches. In this chapter we aim to chronicle the nature of this quite fundamental shift of thinking, and show how it contrasts strongly with the old sceptical mood with regard to healing that has pervaded society and the churches in recent centuries. Because of it, healing has tended to be at best only a fringe activity. Now healing is becoming much more discussed, and indeed the 'man in the street' seems to have an openness to the reality of healing greater than that of many in the churches, who cling on to conservative notions about the nature of God and his unwillingness to interfere in the detail of our day-to-day lives.

The real problem for Church and society in the matter of healing — and this has been perhaps a greater problem for the Church — is that there has been a lack of a consistent language in which to talk about it. One needs a proper conceptual framework for talking about something as elusive as healing, otherwise one is left with a series of anecdotal statements which are totally unconnected with any of the main disciplines of human study. Neither science nor philosophy nor theology have been able to provide a proper framework of concepts and language, and thus communication on the subject of healing has been almost impossible except at the level of sharing human experience. However compelling a particular experience of healing may be for an individual, it has little meaning for those who do not share the world-view of the one recounting the experience. Statements like 'I was healed by God', or 'Jesus removed my limp', are not easily converted into the language of the conventional disciplines of

131

study. Scientists and doctors have found it notoriously difficult to evaluate claims of healing, whether Christian or not. Other explanations have been brought forward to explain the physical improvement of an individual who claims to have been healed by non-medical means.

Theologians also have tended to side with the men of science in preserving a dignified agnosticism as to the reality of the healing ministry in the Church. Even now I am unaware of any teacher of theology at university level who is prepared to speak openly of a belief in the effectiveness of the Church's healing ministry. The official response of the Archbishops' Commission on Healing in 1958 was, as we noted, strangely reluctant to commit itself on the existence of healing gifts and the reality of miraculous healings. However much sound advice it gave on the conduct of a healing ministry, it could be criticized for making the whole of Christian healing seem extremely dull. Healing is so hedged about with qualifications in the report that few people reading it would want to get involved. While statements emerging from Lambeth Conferences since then have always aimed to encourage the healing ministry, there has still been an evident hesitancy on the part of the church establishment and the theological teaching profession to be openly enthusiastic about healing. The Roman Catholic Church has always professed a belief in the reality of Lourdes, and great energy is expended on taking the sick on pilgrimages there. But the reality of healing ministries nearer home does not seem to have occurred to many Roman Catholics. The concentration on the healing efficacy of particular shrines seems to suggest a somewhat impoverished understanding of Christian healing as a whole. As far as the Anglican Church is concerned, it may be noted that Christian healing has yet to penetrate the curricula of most Anglican theological colleges.

I have already expressed my belief that the mood of agnosticism with regard to healing in and outside the Church may be beginning to change. Within the Church the change is taking place quite simply as the result of the need of more and more Christian people to take account of what is actually happening to individuals healed and changed through the ministry of the laying on of hands. Outside the Church, as I have already indicated, a definite shift is taking place in the way that people think about the things that were formerly perceived to be certainties. It is the purpose of this chapter to sketch out first of all something of this broader context, the new movement of the human spirit through which we are living at the moment. It is important to do this because so much of what is happening in the world today can shed some light upon the nature of healing. This new movement of the human spirit has many expressions, but they are united, I believe, in the fact that all of them are in some way a reaction against the permeating influence of the secular movement of thought of the eighteenth century known as the Enlightenment. The Enlightenment, with its emphasis on reason and a no-nonsense approach to religious questions, enabled Western thought to escape finally from the lingering influences of the Middle Ages and to create the modern technological Western world that we all know. But we of the West today, despite all this enormous progress, are arguably in a situation of crisis. Many people note an impoverishment of spirit, a sense of futility and meaninglessness. It is partly because of this atmosphere in Western civilization that a reaction has begun which questions and challenges the philosophical roots of Enlightenment ideas, because these are perceived to be at the heart of our *malaise*.

The challenge to Enlightenment ideas is seen in some of the new political movements, especially the 'Green' parties with their call for the preservation of the environment. It is found in the religious movements of all kinds which stress religious experience and question what they perceive to be the narrow dogmatism and rationalism of the established churches. It is encountered in the holistic health movement, which is a plea for humanity to be preserved in the impersonality of modern technological medicine. We even find some scientists aware that the mystical ideas of the classical Eastern religions provide 'a consistent and relevant philosophical background to the theories of contemporary science'. Finally, in our day we see economics being studied as if people mattered, and not just as a working out of impersonal laws which are fixed by the 'realities' of commercial life. In short, we are living in a world where more and more people are seeking ways of putting the broader human values and concerns into areas of study, technology, and any place from which they had been excluded. One word to describe this approach is 'holistic', a word which implies that disciplines have been too narrowly defined by our prevailing culture. This human personal dimension is needed back in areas of knowledge where the tendency has been to deny personal values in favour of whatever is efficient, powerful and expedient.

The study of Christian healing is illuminated at many points by the new holistic impulse in human knowledge. The new atmosphere that is around should not make us any the less critical of the details of its actual working out in different contexts; but in general we may warmly welcome its overall influence on our society and culture. This chapter is to review and summarize some of these areas of knowledge that relate to our subject of healing. In the first place we shall be looking in more detail at the ideas of the Enlightenment, in reaction to which so many of the new models of knowledge have emerged. Secondly, we shall be reviewing some of the main ideas contained in what is known as holistic medicine, an approach to medicine in which healing has come to have an honourable place. Thirdly, we shall be looking at the study of contemporary physics, which is held by some to undergird what is in essence a religious view of the universe.

The eighteenth-century ideas of the Enlightenment are based on the thinking and philosophy of René Descartes, the philosopher, scientist and mathematician, who lived in the mid-seventeenth century. Descartes provided the theoretical base for a new knowledge, while the following century saw its further working out, in terms not only of scientific discovery but also of its application to such areas as politics and economics. Descartes' first concern was to concentrate on that knowledge which could be shown to be true in a provable way, like mathematics and geometry. He was impressed by this kind of knowledge because it was certain and predictable, and thus could lead to practical results. He took care to separate the observer or experiencing subject from the things that he observed. There was no room in this process of detached observation and measurement for any of the earlier belief systems about the nature of the world that were part of the old map of knowledge. Technology and the scientific exploration of the world became a genuine possibility once these distracting subjective ideas had been removed. Speculation, for example, about the relationship of God to the world had no relevance to the new knowledge. Once the consistency of nature had come to be recognized, such considerations were seen to be unnecessary as a method of explanation. Mathematics, both as a tool of measurement and as a model of truth, was the new feature of this confident rationalism. It was not hard to convince the contemporaries and successors of Descartes that here was knowledge of the highest order. Scientists were set free to examine and measure every aspect of the world of nature, and the success of this approach was seen in the rapid transformation of society in the West, culminating in the technological culture of today.

In this process of measurement and exploration of the natural world, the human species, like everything else, came to be an object of study. It was thought to be only a matter of time before the inexplicable aspects of our nature would come to be understood. Notions of soul and spirit, belonging as they did to belief systems, had no part in the scientific study of humanity, which after Descartes thus came to be a matter of examining our material nature; and human needs were thought of in very materialistic terms. Much political thought of the late eighteenth and nineteenth centuries is marked by an aggressive atheism. Freedom of the individual, for example, was, and is still, sometimes considered to be secondary to the demands of the State, which organizes society in accordance with the laws of a 'scientific' materialism.

The Enlightenment provided a double-edged weapon, with which, on the one hand, it was possible to cut away the superstition and woolly ideas that had marked much of the thinking of previous centuries, and hence to exploit the natural world and create levels of technological success and comfort never before experienced. On the other hand, because it emphasized the supremacy of reason, other aspects of our human nature, the more subtle spiritual levels of personality and the feelings, were less regarded. It is not surprising that the eighteenth century was, at one level, among the most secular periods of history. Not only were the Christian dogmas derided by the intelligentsia — this was not of course the situation among those who listened to Wesley — but the authority of Scripture as making a contribution to truth was almost completely disregarded. The whole traditional Christian presentation of truth seemed to the eighteenth-century 'cultured despiser' as being hopelessly obsolete and unworthy of serious attention. The only religion to survive in the broad consensus of Enlightenment thinking throughout Europe was the rather anaemic belief in God known as Deism. A belief in God was permissible as long as it did not involve accepting the irrational aspects of faith, among which was the belief in miracles. These were thought to be quite impossible, as they suggested a God who intervened in nature in an arbitrary fashion. If God had created the laws through which nature operated, he would in some way be contradicting himself by allowing miracles to take place. The classic refutation of miracles by David Hume was presented on these lines. He declared that miracles were impossible, and that if they were thought to happen, then there was some kind of mistake at work.

Among those who form part of the current reaction against the assumptions of the Enlightenment we look first at a group of doctors organized by the British Holistic Medical Association. We have already encountered many of their ideas in the discussion with Dr Pearce, a founder member of the Association. These doctors are concerned, among other things, about the materialism that has appeared to take over medicine as a legacy of the Enlightenment. Like Dr Pearce they have found themselves able to take seriously the claims of healers, even if they have not looked much to the churches for their understanding of the nature of healing.

Before we look further at the ideas of these holistic doctors, and the way that they have begun to create a language for talking about healing within the framework of their own discipline and training, it will be instructive for us to look at the recent history of the attitude of the medical profession generally towards healing. In 1956 the medical profession in Britain, through the British Medical Association, made a study of healing. Those undertaking this study, which as far as I know has not been superseded, were reluctant in their conclusions to ascribe healing to anything more than a form of suggestion similar to 'other forms of psychological treatment employed by doctors'. The implication was that the BMA simply did not accept that Christian or any other healing could affect a disease which was not in some way psychological in origin. The concept of an external power or energy at work healing the disorder was quite foreign to their thinking, and unacceptable. Clearly what the BMA were pointing to does cover a part of what happens in healing; but, as readers of this book will know, by no means all. At that time the BMA felt it important to present healing as something totally explicable within the framework of psychological studies, and thus in no way upsetting any of the scientific or philosophical presuppositions of the mechanical model of the human organism.

The perspective of the eighties makes the 1956 statement of the BMA look somewhat condescending. In the past thirty years many doctors have come to recognize that there are treatments, such as acupuncture, which show mechanisms at work within the body that operate in ways not easy to explain in terms of the traditional mechanistic way of talking about living organisms. There is now also the philosophical challenge to the medical profession which comes from those who practise holistic medicine, who no longer believe that the mechanical explanations arising out of the Enlightenment can tell us all there is to know about ourselves as human beings. A criticism of medicine for its materialism has been made not only by doctors, but also by the Church. The Church's Council for Health and Healing, founded in 1944 by William Temple, had as one of its aims a dialogue with the medical profession so that they would indeed come to accept this insight, that men and women are far more than just their bodies. But such prophetic ideas have not really penetrated the medical profession, even though many individual doctors may have taken this criticism into their thinking. A materialistic way of thinking has in most areas of medicine continued to reign supreme, and scant regard for what Christians would call people's spiritual nature has been paid, in, for example, the whole massive research programme for the treatment of cancer. Also, one detects little sign yet that medical students are presented with any other model than the materialistic one. But the mood is beginning to change as the media and royal patronage make holistic ideas more commonplace.

The ideas of holistic medicine have to be looked at with interest. Not only is it rediscovering what is in essence a Judaeo/Christian view of humanity, it is also providing a conceptual

137

framework for talking about something that is known and understood by many people, including Christians; namely, healing. The fact that the proponents of holistic medicine are not necessarily Christian in their outlook or presuppositions is no cause for alarm. We must be grateful that the British Holistic Medical Association is providing a forum where the concerns of both doctors and healers can be looked at at the same time. In other words, holistic medicine is prepared and ready to enter into dialogue with Christians involved with healing. While the position on the medical side of the dialogue makes no Christian assumptions, the spiritual nature of man is firmly on the agenda. Nevertheless, at the moment this kind of discussion is not widespread. One is normally made to feel that the contribution of Christians to the work of healing is at best marginal to the real work of medical science. There may well be particular places where such attitudes are not found, but recently a hospital chaplain told me that in the eyes of most of the medical staff his role was to deal with their failures, i.e. death, and the comfort of bereaved relatives. In all the contemporary discussion about co-operation between Church and medicine, one detects that there are still in many places enormous gulfs of communication and understanding.

In the proceedings of the BHMA published in 1984 we can pick up some more of the main lines of this fascinating and important debate. In the first paper, Patrick Pietroni, the Chairman of the Association, sets out the case for Holism as a valid concept in medicine. He lists the fundamental principles on which holistic medicine is based. I have thought it worthwhile to quote these in full.

(1) The human organism is a multidimensional being, possessing body, mind and spirit, all inextricably connected, each part affecting the whole and the whole being greater than the sum of the parts.

(2) There is an inter-connectedness between human beings and their environment which includes other human beings. This inter-connectedness acts as a force on the functioning of the individual isolated human being.

(3) Disease or ill-health arises as a result of a state of imbalance, either from within the human being or because of some external

force in the environment, and by environment I include the family.

(4) We each possess a powerful and innate capacity for healing ourselves, or bringing ourselves back into a state of balance.

(5) One of the primary tasks of someone entrusted to heal, be he doctor, priest or acupuncturist, is to encourage the self-innate capacity for healing of the individual in distress.

(6) This primary task can often be better accomplished through education than through direct intervention, whether that intervention be penicillin, surgery or a homoeopathic prescription.

(7) To enable him to accomplish his task effectively, the healer needs to be aware of his own multi-dimensional levels of existence and have some expertise and ability in achieving a state of balance and state of harmony within himself — 'physician heal thyself'.

Most of these ideas have been encountered in the interview with Dr Pearce, and these principles of Dr Pietroni's are offered to help readers further understand the dynamic of holistic medicine. It should be stressed here quite clearly that the principles of holism are not alternatives to the practice of traditional medicine. Rather, holistic doctors are concerned to widen the outlook of their more orthodox colleagues, by attempting to treat people at every level of their being, and not just at the physical level. For us the important thing is that much of what we have discovered about Christian healing is allowed expression in the new atmosphere that the holistic doctors are trying to promote, where not only can healers find acceptance, but they are considered to be part of the total process of healing that is promoted. Whatever hypothesis is used to explain healing, the healer, Christian or otherwise, is afforded an honourable place by at least one group of medical practitioners.

In his article, Dr Pietroni also takes the reader back to a consideration of the philosophical roots of modern medicine, which, like us, he finds in the scientific and philosophical work of Descartes. As we have seen, Descartes believed that the body could be regarded as an object working in accordance with the same mechanical laws as any other object. He also established the principle that the study of the body could be made by examining all the different parts separately; in other words, that the body is no more than the sum total of all its constituent parts. We have already discussed the Enlightenment which Descartes' ideas made possible. But, as we have also seen, this great movement of modern progress has not been without cost. There has, for example, been a downgrading of some aspects of the human mind — wonder, love, and respect for people and our environment — in favour of the human reason.

The mechanistic model of the human organism is questioned by Pietroni because it fails to do justice to the personality at a pragmatic level. Now it is also under attack from a different quarter. Pietroni in his article points out that the assumptions of Newtonian physics, which are the basis of traditional scientific thought, are no longer held to be ultimate explanations of the nature of the physical world. A new model has emerged with the recognition of some implications of post-Einsteinian physics. We shall be looking at some of these ideas below, but meanwhile we should note the importance of the idea of interconnectedness that Pietroni presents. This is a concept that has currency in the writings of both physicists and holistic doctors. Human beings, like everything else in the universe, are linked to their environment and to other human beings. The understanding of this link with what is beyond us is clearly of vital importance in providing appropriate treatment. Not only has each of us the capacity to heal others in and through our innate interconnectedness with them, but there is also a clear need to remove obstacles to our healing from our surroundings.

The organization of the study of holistic medicine is likely to be of great assistance to the Church as it struggles not only to rediscover its healing ministry but also to find a coherent language with which to talk about it. The language and conceptual framework of the holistic doctors is of course only one way of talking about healing. In no sense would I suggest that there is any ultimate value in the way that holistic doctors are talking, but they do represent an important intellectual movement in the world today, from which the Church can find much help. Given the fact that ten years ago an interest in healing from an academic point of view was even less respectable than it is today, this new ally on the field is greatly to be welcomed. We may not agree in every respect with our new friends, but at least dialogue with them will be dialogue which shares many common ideas, and is not based on the incomprehension that seems to have marked the 1956 report. But before I become too ecstatic about the possibilities for dialogue between the Church and the holistic doctor, there is one cloud on the horizon which must be faced. While holistic doctors are prepared to be positive about healing, they do not in fact look much to the Church when seeking examples of healing. They are much more likely to relate to a body such as the well-organized National Association of Spiritual Healers, which we have already encountered with Dr Pearce. This organization, founded some thirty years ago by the late Harry Edwards, the well-known faith-healer, brings together 'spiritual' healers of all kinds. It also provides professional training and accreditation, and, for many people, not only holistic doctors, is the kind of organization to which one must look to find evidence of healing in this country today. The Church is seen as a relative novice in this whole area of healing. 'Healing' for most people means the work of 'faith healers', and those who call themselves by this name either are not members of the mainstream churches, or at any rate do not see their skill as necessarily deriving from their church membership.

In our brief survey of the thinking of holistic medicine we noted that one of the key ideas of the reaction against the old mechanistic model of medicine was that science itself has undergone a fundamental shift in its self-understanding. Mechanistic theories about the nature of the human organism are seen to be unsatisfactory, not only from the point of view of failing to meet our common-sense criteria about ourselves and our needs, but because they are also seen to fail from the point of view of the new scientific thinking that is around today.

For a book of this kind to embark on any kind of discussion of post-Einsteinian physics might seem foolhardy in the extreme, but for the fact that a number of books have appeared in the last ten years that have attempted to make this subject accessible to the layman. These books have been written not only so that the non-scientist can be initiated into abstruse and highly technical arguments, but because the findings of the new physics are believed to be relevant to all of us, and to our thinking and perception of the world. In brief the old common-sense perception of the physical world, which is based on trust in the senses, and on some appreciation of Newtonian laws of motion and cause and effect, is held to be incomplete. While the traditional physics is able to explain a wide range of natural phenomena, it breaks down when faced with the activity and unpredictable behaviour of particles at a sub-atomic level. The discoveries of Einstein, that space and time are inextricably bound up together, and the observations by nuclear physicists of the workings of the sub-atomic world, mean that science can no longer be appealed to as having a clear objective understanding of the truth about the natural world. Expressions like 'uncertainty principle' and 'tendencies to occur' have crept into the discussions of the behaviour of sub-atomic particles. In short, the confidence of science that it was able to explain totally the workings of the natural world has given way to a new realism and a recognition that the best that can be achieved are provisional models about how nature functions at sub-atomic levels. These fall far short of the old objective mathematical explanations of reality handed down to us by Newton and his successors.

The new atmosphere of humility in scientific explanations has been around for quite some time, but it is only recently that this has become known to those outside the scientific community. In a recent article in the magazine *Christian*, James Lambert, a scientist, looks at the book *The Myth of God Incarnate* and criticizes the way it is basing its ideas of what is 'true' in a theological context on obsolete scientific theories. He criticizes the idea that if a 'myth' is not literally true, it can no longer be accepted as valid. He also questions the common assumption that the idea of supernatural causation is no longer scientifically acceptable. Dr Lambert's argument against the first assumption rests on the fact that science encounters reality using models and analogy. Literal fact is not what the scientist is finding. For example, light can be explained as waves, but this does not explain every phenomenon about light. Another theory or model of light is that a ray of light is analogous to a stream of machine-gun bullets. Logically, Dr Lambert points out, these two explanations are inconsistent. It cannot be literally true that light is both things simultaneously. Dr Lambert regards religious statements as having a similar function, in that they are not literally true, but nevertheless they reveal something of God. He quotes with approval Thomas Aquinas, who declared, 'Those things which are said of God and other things are predicated neither univocally nor equivocally but analogically.' He sums up the whole of this part of the argument in this way: 'Neither scientist nor theologian believes that the theories and doctrines are factually and literally true, but they are the best working models available, we have to use them to order our lives and experience, and we know that they work.'

Dr Lambert then goes on to discuss another inbuilt assumption of the 'myth' debate, which is that supernatural causation is an impossible idea for modern scientific man to accept. Again, looking at the new insights of physics, he notes that there is an inbuilt unpredictability in the behaviour of a single particle, even if the behaviour of trillions of particles can be seen as largely coherent and predictable, through an averaging-out process. The unpredictability of a single particle is similar to the unpredictability of actual events as we experience them in the course of our day-to-day lives. Scientists talk in terms of broad probabilities, not in terms of the actual events that in fact happen. For example, it can be predicted how many people will move house in any particular year, even though not which people. Dr Lambert believes it to be perfectly reasonable to see in the chances and changes of our personal and national histories the hand of God at work. This is the actual claim of many Christians in practice, and scientists go beyond their competence if they try to pretend that this is impossible. It is a misleading claim to see the events of history or nature as being totally fixed and determined, just as it is mistaken to regard scientific statements about sub-atomic matter as being literally and objectively true.

Dr Lambert's article is typical of a new mood of humility that is affecting many physicists today with regard to their work. Gone are the hard certainties that marked the traditional science which descends from Isaac Newton. His observations of course continue to be true within the context of certain experimental situations, but the Newtonian laws break down and are inapplicable when we look either at objects moving at the speed of light, or at sub-atomic levels. Among the insights that are revealed to us by the nuclear physicists on the nature of matter,

Dr Lambert has shown us two. First, he has indicated that what is revealed to the observer will depend on what he is looking for. He will 'see' light as waves or machine-gun bullets according to which experiment is set up. It is thus hard, and many writers point this out, to speak of an objective reality which is separate from the observer after the Cartesian pattern. In this way the notion of the detached observer is a myth. The second phenomenon that Dr Lambert has referred to is the unpredictability of the behaviour of sub-atomic particles. This again is different from the Newtonian laws of cause and effect with which we are so familiar, even if only from a common-sense point of view.

A third insight from the writers on modern physics is the notion that the only way of understanding the universe is to see it in its totality. This insight is arrived at from the observation that phenomena at the sub-atomic level are more to be explained in terms of their relationships and interconnectedness than as separately existing objects such as we deal with in the sensory world. One writer has summed it up by saying, 'An elemental particle is not an independently existing unanalysable entity. It is, in essence, a set of relationships that reach outward to other things.' Another writer, David Bohm, goes further in his famous statement that, 'Everything in the universe implicates everything else.'

This review of modern ideas of physics is of necessity brief, partly because in these matters I very soon find myself getting out of my depth, and partly because the detailed arguments of the physicists are not of prime concern to the argument of this book. Enough has been said to give something of the flavour of the way in which contemporary physicists are speaking about their researches. Also, it is important for readers to recognize that these discoveries, as a whole plethora of writers never tire of telling us, have important implications for our philosophy and way of looking at the world. One theme that is taken up, by Fritjof Capra among others, is that the new description of the universe and of man's place in it reads very much like the classical Eastern mystical view of reality. Although they start from very different standpoints and frameworks, both mystics and physicists have an apprehension of the oneness of the universe and of our intimate participation in it.

The old mystical statements about the unknowability of God also appear to be paralleled in the way that the description of particles goes beyond the conceptual framework of human understanding. But here our interest is to sketch out briefly how healing appears to fit into the strange world that is glimpsed by the nuclear physicist. The world we have seen through his eyes is a world of far more complex interconnections that we normally perceive. Healing is then perhaps partly to be understood as the restoring of what is broken between one human being and another, and between human beings and the universe as a whole. This is picking up the language of LeShan as we saw it in the last chapter, but it appears aptly relevant in this strange world-view that we have briefly entered. It is widely recognized that illness may be some kind of failure of adaptation to the environment. At a higher or deeper level illness may be a 'wrongness' in relation to the universe as a whole. Healing would thus quite naturally take on a cosmic dimension, as LeShan has described. We need to be shifted out of a negative relationship into a new positive life-enhancing relationship with reality as a whole. To do this we need to be helped by someone who is already 'at-one' with the Cosmos, or God.

The evaluation of healing by contemporary scientists is likely to be far more pragmatic and less condemnatory than it has been by scientists who were able to operate only from the perspective of Newtonian physics. There is already, as we have seen, a readiness by holistic doctors to accept healing as a fact, even if they are not able to explain how it works. By moving from a need to find explanations of a literal kind to the positing of models of how it appears to work, the contemporary scientist can approach healing with a great deal more humility. Such scientists are still in the minority, but healing may reasonably expect from now on to be taken seriously by some scientists. The shift away from mechanistic explanations of the human condition means that even the parapsychological aspects of it are now being taken a good deal more seriously by researchers. The laws of nineteenth-century physics held that psychic abilities could not exist, and therefore were fraudulent. Some present-day Christians go further, and appear to use those nineteenth-century mechanical laws as the criteria of what is acceptable and what is occult and forbidden. There is now the recognition that our apparent ability to cross time and space with our minds may cohere with the new picture of the universe offered us by the physicist. The exact explanation of how we sometimes experience things 'psychically', in ways that go beyond our ordinary physical senses, has still a long way to go. But we may find that within a generation, people will regard as normal and natural those things in us which are now considered by many to be mysterious, occult and forbidden. Healing implies at the very least an interchange of energy between one person and another which has nothing to do with physical energy.

The new atmosphere and mood of scientific research will lead, one would hope, to a more holistic way of studying healing events. Anyone who has experienced a healing knows perfectly well that the incident was far more than just a physical change in their condition. For every healing there is a whole context of events and experiences all of which make up the total event. To regard the actual physical change as the only important fact is hardly to do justice to the healing. Time and time again in the past, miracles and healings have been written off as spontaneous remissions and psychologically-induced changes, because in the mind of the investigator that was the only possible explanation. Perhaps it will always be true that the physical aspect of a healing will defy the kind of proof that nineteenth-century physics, with its built-in scepticism, demands. The medical bureau at Lourdes picks up only a fraction of those who have been helped. Perhaps they are asking the questions which fit in only with the now out-moded scientific point of view. The 'literal' healing totally misses out of account what is perhaps more important, for the patient anyway: that is, the spiritual transformation that may have been experienced. But where the questions embrace a wider vision of reality, the patient's state of mind and readiness to deal with guilt, the spiritual and psychic abilities of the healer, and the interaction between the two, then we shall find healings being evaluated better. In the first evaluation, only one part of the healing event is being analysed, and that in accordance with one understanding of what is possible. In the second, an attempt is being made to view the event from a holistic perspective, by trying to hold every aspect of it together. The subjective experience of the healing is also considered as being part of the whole occurrence. The fact that the event may not be able to be totally explained does not mean that it is written off as impossible. The 'humble' investigator will seek to evaluate, not only the event itself, but all that flows out of it in terms of the changed perceptions of the world in those who were participants in it. The humble holistic investigator is not going to be any more gullible in the face of fraud, but he is certainly going to start from a position of sympathy rather than one of cynical scepticism.

NINE

Towards a Theology of Healing — Holistic Theology?

The struggle for Christian healing to be taken seriously by the men of science is paralleled in a most extraordinary way in its relationship to traditional theology. Morton Kelsey has chronicled this unexpected situation, and it would be useful to look at his findings before we look at some ideas of my own about a possible way out of the theological *impasse*.

In his book *Healing and Christianity*, Kelsey presents what he describes as the case against Christian healing. He notes the implicit teaching of the Book of Common Prayer in its Office for the Visitation of the Sick. The prayers indicate a belief not in healing but in the corrective role of sickness. One prayer observes that sickness may be sent to 'try your patience for the example of others . . . or else it be sent unto you to correct and amend in you whatsoever doth offend the eyes of your heavenly Father.' The sick person is also called upon to 'render unto him humble thanks for his fatherly visitation.' Kelsey comments that although the Office is rarely if ever used, the ideas contained in it remain a powerful force in the thinking of many people. He summarizes the ideas which are contained in the Office and which remain typical of much Protestant thinking today.

(1) God is responsible for sickness.

(2) Sickness is seen as punishment by God, though it is chastisement by a God who loves us.

(3) God sends sickness to show people that they have sinned, so as to enable repentance to take place, as well as to try their patience and enable them to grow in holiness.

(4) The role of the minister is to preserve the spiritual health and soul of the sick by exhorting them to confession. Thus there is no healing role at all for the Christian minister.

Another theme within Protestant theology noted by Kelsey is that of dispensationalism. This idea was expressed by both Luther and Calvin, and according to it the miracles of the time of Christ and the apostles were for the building up of the Church at that time only, 'but to us . . . no such powers have been committed.' Kelsey notes that a modern Protestant giant, Barth, avoids any extensive discussion of healing, either to affirm it or deny it. Another recent author is mentioned, Dr Wade Boggs. In his *Faith Healing and the Christian Faith*, Dr Boggs reproduces the old dispensational idea. When faced with the need to account for Pentecostal and other forms of healing that were in fact being practised, Dr Boggs found ways of ridiculing the style in which these healings were conducted; thus the healings themselves were seen as ridiculous. Kelsey notes that as recently as 1962 two-and-a-half million Lutherans in America were warned to steer clear of religious healing.

The final strand of theology that Kelsey examines is that of Christian existentialism. He notes the antipathy of such writers as Husserl and Kierkegaard to the supernatural, either as historical revelation or as a present experienced reality. He goes on to note Bultmann's complete disregard for any objective reality in the Gospel accounts of Jesus's healing. If they did not happen then, there is no reason to expect them to happen now. If a person believes them to happen now he is clearly 'under the domination of a "mythological" point of view which is untenable in the modern world'.

I have glanced briefly at the points raised by Kelsey to indicate a basic antipathy shown towards religious healing by Protestant theologians. Indeed not only theologians but also the typical Protestant believer is more than likely to have picked up some such sentiments as those embodied in the Book of Common Prayer, and made them part of his mental furniture. A deeper theological objection to Christian healing is, however, found in a much older debate, one that goes back to the time of Thomas Aquinas in the thirteenth century.

The philosophical thinking of the ancient world was dominated by the figure of Plato, who died at the end of the fourth century BC. His ideas went through many changes and transformations and thus it is difficult to talk about Platonism as though it were a single philosophy. There are, however, one or two themes that recur in every expression of this philosophy. One conviction is the belief in a higher reality transcending the present world of sense experience, but it is one which it is possible to penetrate. The task of describing how to penetrate that world was given to mystical theology or spirituality. There were also certain cultic methods available to those who wished to ascend into the world beyond. Speaking very generally, it could be claimed that Eastern Orthodoxy has preserved the ethos of Platonism; Christian theology is much more a matter of spirituality than of intellectual speculation. Indeed one eminent author on Orthodoxy claims that theology and spirituality are one.

The Western attitude to theology, as formulated by St Thomas Aquinas, has very different roots. His inspiration was Aristotle, a near contemporary of Plato who had opposed much of what the master taught. While Plato had taught that every object and reality conformed to and participated in a transcendent 'idea' or 'form', Aristotle opposed this idea. For him, man lived in a closed universe into which there was nothing that could penetrate. This was rather similar to the eighteenth-century ideas about the immutable laws of nature operating without interference. God came to be more a logical idea than a perceived or experienced reality.

Aristotle's ideas were never very popular in the ancient world, presumably because they conflicted with the prevailing ethos of man's religious imagination, which felt the transcendent world very close. But his style of argument went down very well in the setting of the early universities, the setting of Aquinas's theological work. There the emphasis was on the need to know, using precise and confident logical arguments. Platonism, in contrast, what little of it was available to the early medievals, seemed vague and woolly by comparison. Aquinas's introduction of many of the basic ideas of Aristotle into his great masterpiece, the *Summa Theologica*, was a resounding success. The *Summa* became a massive influence on the Western Church, and its style of argument and method of presenting theology is not without its admirers even today. But within this system, healing had a hard task to survive at all. Because the world was assumed to be a coherent and consistent place, healings and miracles had to be extraordinary if they happened at all. The fact that miracles and healings went on happening throughout the Middle Ages was an indication that the vast mass of people knew nothing of the abtruse arguments of the scholastic theologians, and continued to experience God in their own way. In Aquinas's own writings the emphasis was on God's spiritual work with men, and Christ's ministry had nothing whatever to do with the body, even in spite of the accounts of miracles. Where these were discussed they were seen to demonstrate Christ's power and divinity. '. . . Christ, by miraculously healing men in particular, should prove himself to be the universal and spiritual Saviour of all.' Aquinas also made his priorities very clear when he said: 'By how much a soul is of more account than a body, by so much is the forgiving of sins a greater work than the healing the body . . .'

We can see now that healing as a theological idea fitted badly into the framework of theological orthodoxy, since it has been denied by both the main Western systems of theology, Catholic and Protestant. The basic problem, as I see it, is that theology in the West since the time of Aquinas has allowed itself to become a coherent system of intellectual knowledge which is not properly integrated into the whole area of religious experience of which healing is one expression. Religious experiences, however much they are part of the gospel proclamation, are excluded because they inconveniently do not fit into the pattern of logic and coherence that is at the heart of theological method.

Readers who have travelled this far with me will, I hope, feel some sympathy when I say bluntly that if a theological system cannot accommodate the reality of Christian healing, then there is something wrong with the theology. Of all the main traditions of the Christian world, Eastern Orthodox theology alone might have provided a theological language for talking about the reality of Christian healing. There is in that tradition, as we have seen, a bias towards Platonism with its openness to the transcendent. It is in Orthodox theology that we encounter such doctrines as the 'divinization' of humanity, the transfiguration of humanity, body and soul. Also, Orthodoxy is deeply conscious of the ultimate transfiguration of the material world, and this is proclaimed in the use of icons. According to an Orthodox writer, the icon is 'a concrete example of matter restored to its original harmony and beauty . . . The icons were part of the transfigured cosmos.' One could wish that Orthodox theologians were more conscious of the reality of healing in the Church's life. There is no doubt that their theological conceptual framework would not in itself prove an obstacle as it has done in the West.

Returning to the West again, we have already noted the Aristotelian bias that leaves healing out on a limb. Now we need to recognize another all-pervading influence on modern Western theology that again inhibits the ready acceptance of Christian healing. The influence I refer to is once again the all-pervading Enlightenment. We have already given an example in the previous chapter of the way that eighteenth-century ideas of truth affect the presuppositions and ideas of a modern book, *The Myth of God Incarnate*. If Dr Lambert's argument about the use of 'myth' stands, then we can see that many of the current controversies in the Church have a peculiarly old-fashioned ring. The whole debate about the place of theology in a world dominated by Enlightenment presuppositions is also taken up in another widely-acclaimed book, *The Other Side of 1984* by Lesslie Newbigin. Newbigin's argument and analysis of the present climate of Christian theology is one that we need to spend some time considering, since his concerns are not so far removed from the concerns of this book.

The short analysis and description of the Enlightenment that is presented by Newbigin, is one of the best available. He well captures, in a quotation of d'Alembert written in 1759, the enormous sense of confidence generated by the new thought of the mid-eighteenth century. The old authorities of Revelation gave way to the new authorities of 'observable facts'. The old disciplines of law, politics, art and history were removed from their association with metaphysics and theology, and left to work out rules for their study in accordance with the new independent spirit of enquiry. In relation to this fresh spirit of confidence, the dogmatic claims of the Church about truth seemed tired and old-fashioned.

Newbigin acknowledges the enormous debt of our civilization to the movement of the Enlightenment, but, like many modern commentators, he also notes how the 'liberation' of the reason from old-fashioned dogma has not achieved its promise. Scientific explanations, he points out, do not satisfy at deeper levels of meaning, and it is impossible for anyone to function without a system of 'belief' with which to interpret the world, though he is not here talking about religious belief. He struggles to restate the place of Christian 'dogma' in the modern world, without its being seen as a reaffirmation of dogmatism, which has, rightly he thinks, been rejected. Newbigin is not at his clearest when talking about 'dogma'. He seems to be referring to the Christian framework of belief and trust in the Kingdom, the proclamation that God is in the midst of history and Lord of every part of life. He wants to explore how this can be affirmed and articulated in the world without its seeking the kind of dominance that it achieved under Constantine; it is to have the quality of real dialogue with other frameworks of belief, 'fiduciary frameworks', as he calls them. The dialogue is to have the quality of vulnerability, which is a mark of its commitment — 'a commitment which always means risking everything'.

Part of the Enlightenment's legacy to the Church has been to push it off into the 'private' and marginal side of life and leave the rest of life, especially the political and economic decision-making, to those who are 'expert' in these areas. Newbigin does not of course accept this marginalization of Christianity, and part of his plea to the churches is to challenge the economic and political structures, as well as questioning the whole Enlightenment framework that has proclaimed human autonomy in these areas. In engaging in this 'missionary encounter' the Church recognizes that it offers 'a "fiduciary framework" quite different from and (in some respects) incompatible with the framework within which modern European culture has developed'. He recalls a previous occasion when the Church sought to proclaim the Kingdom of God in a world that rejected its claim. The Roman Empire possessed all the might of political power while the Church had only 'the word of testimony and the faithfulness of the martyrs'. But the weapons of the Church proved stronger, and the whole Roman world surrendered to the Lordship of Christ. Newbigin acknowledges that the current encounter with society cannot be on a Constantinian basis, rather he sees a 'discipleship . . . to make visible that understanding and ordering of life which takes as its "fiduciary framework" the revelation of himself that God has given in Jesus.' This is a very different vocation for the Church from that left to it by society, namely to be concerned with the cultivation of the soul and affairs of eternity. Newbigin is all the time trying to recover the vision of Christianity that he perceives in the New Testament, a faith that is concerned for the whole of life. It cannot be simply watered down to suit the mood of the culture, but rather must rediscover its inherent vocation to relate to the whole of man's experience.

As I understand Newbigin, he seems to be calling for a new way of doing theology in the modern day. In the first place he is asking for a theology that embraces every area of human life, while simultaneously not falling into the trap of setting itself up over other expressions of truth, as light against darkness. The three words that sum up his approach are 'holistic', 'vulnerable' and 'humble'. 'Dogma' is thus found, not in a series of propositions, but in the encounter with the Kingdom of God as revealed in Christ. In other words, theology is not to be confined to propositional statements or certain limited areas of life. He demands a theology that breaks out of all the limits that we put on it, both of language and of application.

I have given considerable space to outlining Newbigin's analysis and ideas because in many ways I have myself arrived at a position parallel to his. For him theology has been found wanting in that it often fails to engage the political and economic issues of our time. Theology for me is found wanting in so far as it fails to grapple with the reality of God's contemporary revelation of himself, of which healing is a powerful example. The reason for both these failures is that theology has allowed itself to be limited and restricted by the philosophy of the Enlightenment and hence to become a marginal activity.

I would match Newbigin's plea for Christians to engage in the area of political and economic issues with a plea for theology to engage properly with the reality of healing. We both seek a freedom for theology from the shackles of Enlightenment ideas. I have already indicated something of the direction in which Newbigin is moving in his attempt to allow theology to engage in wider issues. We have called this theology that is concerned with the whole 'holistic', and have noted other characteristics, namely its humility and vulnerability. For the rest of this chapter, I think it important to work out further what might be the characteristics of this 'holistic' theology, a theology that not only refuses to accept for itself the post-Enlightenment assumptions about its role on the periphery of knowledge, but is also for us rooted in the experiences of healing and wholeness in the widest sense. Although Newbigin's particular concerns with society and our interest in wholeness and healing may appear different, perhaps they do not ultimately diverge from one another very much. His ideas will of course continue to assist us, particularly his ideas about the use and misuse of Scripture. But our presentation of 'holistic theology' will mainly start from ideas that belong to the central themes of this book.

The task of describing the characteristics of 'holistic' theology is an ambitious one, and we can do no more than present an outline of what theology might be, once freed from Enlightenment shackles. Newbigin has given three characteristics from which to begin to build up this idea. Others no doubt will continue the process of describing how theology is to be studied and taught in an age when Enlightenment ideas are no longer accepted without question.

(1) In making a statement about God or articulating a religious truth of any kind, theologians, or indeed any Christians, must speak with humility. They must realize that whatever language they use is of a provisional kind. In this they take account of the revolution in physics after Einstein, and the difficulty there is of making 'objective' statements. Others may prefer to use a different set of concepts. If these convey to other people what is recognizably an encounter with the Kingdom of God, then an attitude of respect is in order.

(2) The Kingdom of God, the encounter with God through the risen Christ in his healing, forgiving and loving movement towards humankind, is at the heart of the distinctive Christian experience. It can be seen to impinge on every area of human life, including the social, political and economic areas of society.

(3) There is a profound simplicity in the basic apprehension of the Christian gospel. Jesus's words about entering the Kingdom as a child remain true. Our tendency to rationalize and verbalize everything to do with Christianity has made our faith a highly

cerebral thing. In the difficulty and complexity of applying the Christian faith to life, we have lost sight of the simplicity of the basic experience. Faith in God involves mind, emotions and the body. It is about opening the whole of ourselves up as much as possible to the reality of God and his Spirit in our lives.

(4) Holistic theology in its dialogue with other ideologies and ideas is unwilling to condemn outright another person's idea of God. As it is based on a living experience of God's activity, the Kingdom, and not on a series of logically-defined propositions, it will try to identify with whatever is placed before it in humility and understanding. Where there is no possibility of mutual understanding, silence may be a more appropriate gesture than condemnation. Holistic theology will always in the process of dialogue question the unspoken assumptions of the other side and allow its own assumptions to be questioned.

(5) Holistic theology, being rooted in an encounter with the healing, loving and forgiving power of God in Christ, is never threatened by others. It is rooted not in argument but in love and experience, and therefore is not afraid of those who would seek to ridicule it on intellectual grounds. On the other hand, holistic theologians will try to learn from whatever expression of truth is presented to them with all the intellectual rigour of which they are capable. They never stop learning.

(6) Alongside the humility to which holistic theologians are called, they are also called to vulnerability. It is as Christians come to know their need of God, and experience grief, pain or persecution, that they can assimilate the gospel most readily. Pride, intellectual arrogance and self-sufficiency of all kinds are conversely the most effective barriers to the reception of the gospel.

(7) The life and faith of Christian believers is at all times informed and imbued by the Holy Spirit. By this we do not mean that every Christian must be a formal charismatic, though this is not excluded. Christians know the reality of living within the will of God. Their life is a working out of that will as directed at them personally and at the life of the Christian community to which they belong.

(8) The experience of healing and wholeness points to the truth that God is deeply involved with his creation, that he wills

wholeness and perfection not only for human beings but also for the whole material universe. Holistic theology looks for and expects to witness the power of God breaking through to restore all that is broken, fragmented and divided. Christians are agents in this process, through their prayer and activity.

The eight hallmarks of the theological approach that I have chosen to call holistic sum up very well the position of many of the people who are presented in this book. Even when I detected a strongly fundamentalist creed, this position was subservient to a simple, humble acceptance of the power of God at work in their lives, and to their readiness to live in obedience to his perceived will. The two people who, in totally different contexts, capture this holistic attitude most clearly are Roy Lawrence and Jim Sepulveda. Roy had reached a complete simplicity in his aproach to the healing ministry, though he had travelled the route of a sophisticated Anglican training to arrive where he was. He discovered that the basic truth of the fact 'that Jesus makes a difference' was of far more importance than churchy 'shibboleths'. Simplicity was a hall-mark of his preaching, and we noted that he used no prepared text on his frequent evangelistic invitations. What he carried into the pulpit with him was not a series of intellectually defined propositions, but an experienced reality which needed only to be unpacked and shared with his audience.

The approach of Jim Sepulveda to teaching and preaching was again of almost naive simplicity. The message that he wanted to communicate again and again was simply that God is powerful and loving. He totally lacked evangelical jargon, but through his transparency and openness to God, power seemed to flow through him to reach every corner of his audience. Jim's route to total and utter simplicity was a way that never had to face sophisticated theological teaching. He was innocent of higher criticism, the debates about the date of the earliest Gospel. It is hard to see that such knowledge could have increased his capacity to love and reveal the power of God for people's lives.

All the people interviewed for this book partake, I believe, of the characteristics of holistic theology as I have attempted to define it. It is true of myself and my wife that, as we develop in our healing ministry, our apprehension of the gospel becomes simultaneously simpler and deeper. We also find that our counselling of individuals becomes very uncomplicated, because we leave the complicated bits for God to sort out. In this we may be cutting across the wisdom of professional counselling, but in the innocence that seems to have been given to us, we believe that God is in control of the whole situation and does not require us to do all the work. Prayer, as we have seen, cuts short the whole psychotherapeutic process in a most remarkable way.

One final task remains before we leave this consideration of holistic theology. We need to look at the theological situation of our own time and see how the idea of holism in theology fits into the debates and controversies of our divided churches.

One church that would appear to absorb the idea of holism with great ease would be the Orthodox Church. In my first attempt on this chapter I assembled a considerable amount of material to demonstrate this point. Orthodoxy in its dependence on Platonic thought has a natural sense of the nearness and accessibility of God. It also has a deep awareness of the inherent unity of the transcendent and the earthly, and the capacity of matter, both human and inanimate, to participate in the divine. The tradition of icons, with their portrayal of the transfigured and redeemed bodies of the saints, points to the expectation of the final redemption of the material universe at the *parousia* or Second Coming. The Orthodox Liturgy proclaims all this to its worshippers with great power. And yet amid all the glory of the Orthodox faith, one thing is lacking which makes it less than truly holistic. The Orthodox Church has taken into its structures a defensiveness and intolerance of other faiths which makes it less than humble. However much individuals tread the path of humility within its communion, and of these there are many, the Church itself has little understanding of true dialogue and humility before those who express truth in a different way. The way to which holistic theology points us is a proclamation of truth that is able to include rather than exclude others.

In the West the preoccupations of the churches are somewhat different. We seem to swing between fundamentalisms of various kinds and radical reinterpretations of the faith that verge on denying it altogether. The biblical fundamentalism of the Christian West is, as Lesslie Newbigin points out, itself not a reaffirmation of biblical truth but a projection of Enlightenment ideas onto the Bible. The very expression 'verbal inerrancy' indicates an interest in making scientific assertions of a kind which have little to do with the spirit of Scripture. And yet Christians of a fundamentalist turn of mind sometimes appear to penetrate the heart of the gospel in a way that leaves other more 'sophisticated' Christians behind. But this does not prove the fundamentalists' presuppositions right — merely that their intellectual naivety has allowed them to find the simplicity of the faith far more quickly than those of broader insights. One might feel tempted to commend fundamentalism in spite of its intellectual suicide and ultimate dependence on eighteenth-century ideas. But it trespasses against our holistic ideal in a second way, namely in its sometimes crude defensiveness and intolerance towards those who question its ideas.

The Charismatic Movement again appears to possess many features of holism within its theology. It understands the whole openness to the Holy Spirit and the consequent importance of inner experience in the lives of Christians. But here again it is very often flawed by sectarianism, pride and intolerance. I do not believe that its fundamentalism in scriptural interpretation is so much of a block as it can be among non-charismatic evangelicals. The common awareness of the work of the Spirit seems often to override the need to keep close to a party line on scriptural interpretation. It is here in spite of the flaws that the holistic theologian might find himself most at home.

In the Church of England, outside the confident fundamentalists of both the Anglo-Catholic and the Evangelical variety, there appear to be a large number of Christians whose faith is very fearful, and thus non-holistic in nature. This has been brought out into the open in the somewhat hysterical reaction to comments by the Bishop of Durham. The Bishop's opponents seem not only fearful but also extremely vulnerable in the non-holistic sense. When one hears of people who cease to be Christians because of the apparent disbelief of a bishop, one has to ask what was there to begin with. The Bishop of Durham is himself not immune from criticism from the holistic perspective. One would prefer that he began by explaining to people the nature of the encounter with God in Christ, before blinding them with questions that are of interest only from a post-Enlightenment standpoint. On the other hand, holistic theologians are also going to be highly suspicious of responses to the Bishop which are affirmations of truth that use the language of nineteenth-century physics. The tomb may indeed have been empty, but we are not thereby committed to a belief in a resuscitated corpse, which seems to be the only answer available from the old and now obsolete scientific model. I have not read enough in the new physics to suggest an alternative model, but I am sure there are some more interesting theories on the significance of the empty tomb. If one has a commitment, faith, and experience of the Risen Christ in his healing and saving power, which is where the holistic theologian begins, then all the speculation is anyway only going to be of secondary interest. One also knows that the possibilities open to our speculation today about what happened to the body of Jesus are far more interesting than those glimpsed under the rules and regulations of nineteenth-century physics.

When I began this book some nine months ago, I thought only in terms of the impact of Christian healing on pastoral practice and priorities. Now I have glimpsed a higher and more radical confrontation with the pattern of Christian life today — the impact on Christian theology. For me personally, the experience of healing, and of the Kingdom of God that lies behind it, is absolutely central to my theological and pastoral thinking. And yet I would not be guilty of thinking of healing purely in personal individual terms. As Morris Maddocks indicates in his book, *The Christian Healing Ministry*, healing stretches out to embrace society as a whole. Individual lives are changed by the encounter with the Kingdom, as physical lives are made whole and simultaneously the brokennesses of guilt and sin are healed. One would also hope to see that quality of Kingdom wholeness affecting others. At the heart of the healing experience there is a new orientation with God and an experience of his Kingdom breaking through with forgiveness and salvation in its train. Just as every individual lives within a nexus of relationships, so one would hope and look for a transformation in the quality of those relationships when once the Kingdom has touched the individual. The experience of the Kingdom is also given to groups of people, especially those who pray together for its coming, whether or not

160

it is manifested as healing and wholeness. We must expect and look for the Kingdom to catch up into itself not only individuals, but also groups, communities, and finally whole nations. The Kingdom will be expressed, not by everyone's obeying a particular law, however high and perfect this law might be. It will be seen in the common openness to the power and love of God of every individual, in perfect conformity to his will and in transformed personal attitudes to other people. While this may sound like an impossible Utopia, at least the experience of healing shows that, as far as individuals and groups are concerned, the Kingdom in all its gracious power does come. May more and more be caught up in the Kingdom, the place where God's will is being fulfilled for the whole world.

My earnest hope is that readers of these pages will have picked up something of the excitement of discovery that I myself have experienced in making this study. It has been for me an experience of growth, both in a theological and a spiritual way. From the way that healing has entered into the consciousness of many Christians, it would appear that we are witnessing a rediscovery of the enormous power and resources of the living God for the Church of our time. One might even compare it to that power known to the Church in New Testament times. Perhaps I have in a small way opened the eyes of my readers to this happening. If so, then the book will have achieved something of the purpose for which it was written.

Further Reading

The following are books cited in the text (in order of reference), and others recommended for further reading.

Chapter 1

Bennett, D. J., *Nine O'Clock in the Morning*. Coverdale 1971.
Kelsey, M. T., *Healing and Christianity*. SCM Press 1973.

Chapter 2

MacManaway, B., and Turcan, J., *Healing, the Energy that can Restore Health*. Thorsons 1983. A parallel but very different healing ministry from that of Gibson. Spiritualist in tone.
The Church's Ministry of Healing, Report of the Archbishops' Commission. Church Information Board 1958. See text for comments. A dull, worthy report which does not really engage many of the issues. Needs to be up-dated.

Chapter 3

MacNutt, F., *Healing*. Ave Maria Press 1974.
MacNutt, F., *The Power to Heal*. Ave Maria Press 1977.
MacNutt, F., *The Prayer that Heals*. Hodder & Stoughton 1982. Deceptively simple but highly recommended. It summarizes the best of MacNutt's earlier books.
McAll, K., *Healing the Family Tree*. Sheldon Press 1982.

Chapter 4

Lawrence, R., *Christian Healing Rediscovered*. Kingsway 1976.
Lawrence, R., *Invitation to Healing*. Kingsway 1979.
Cosslett, N., *His Healing Hands*. Hodder & Stoughton 1985.

Further Reading

Chapter 5

Pearce, I., *The Gate of Healing*. Neville Spearman 1983.
Pearce, I., *The Holistic Approach to Cancer*. R. Findlay 1983.
Freeman, H. E., *Angels of Light?* Logos 1969.
Weldon, J., and Levitt, Z., *Psychic Healing*. Moody Press 1982.
Livesey, R., *Understanding Alternative Medicine*. Life Changing Books 1985.
   The last three titles are negative exposés of all things psychic from Conservative Evangelical authors. See chapter 7 for discussion of Livesey's book.
Heaney, J., *The Sacred and the Psychic*. Paulist Press 1984. A more positive account of the 'psychic' problem.

Chapter 6

Peter Scothern has published various pamphlets and booklets which are obtainable from Voice of Deliverance, 84 Church Drive, Quedgeley, Gloucester GL2 6UF.
Don Martin has made several tapes which are obtainable from Ark Tapes, N. C. Arnold, Lower Common, Gilwern, Abergavenny.
Buckingham, J., *Daughter of Destiny*. Logos 1976. This and other books by and about Kathryn Kuhlman may be consulted to capture the flavour of this kind of ministry.
Casdorph, H. R., *Miracles*. Logos 1976. Contains a medical account of Kuhlman's ministry.

Chapter 7

LeShan, L., *The Clairvoyant Reality*. Turnstone 1981.
Benson, H., *The Relaxation Response*. New York 1975.
Benson, H., *Beyond the Relaxation Response*. Fount 1985.
Griffiths, B., *The Marriage of East and West*. Fount 1983.
Griffiths, B., *The Golden String*. Fount 1964.
Johnstone, W., *Silent Music*. Fount 1977.
Johnstone, W., *The Wounded Stag*. Fount 1985.
Johnstone, W., *The Mirror Mind*. Fount 1983.
de Mello, A., *Sadhana − A Way to God*. Anand Press 1978.
Martin, D., and Mullen, D., ed., *Strange Gifts?* Basil Blackwell 1984.

Chapter 8

Capra, F., *The Tao of Physics*. Flamingo 1983.

Capra, F., *The Turning Point*. Flamingo 1983.
Zukav, G., *The Dancing Wu Li Masters*. Flamingo 1984.
Lambert, J., 'A Scientist looks at the Myth' (*Christian*, Vol. 9, No. 3).
Lunn, P., 'New Physics and Old Mystics' (*Christian*, Vol. 9, No. 3).

Chapter 9

Newbigin, L., *The Other Side of 1984*. Risk Books 1983.
Maddocks, M., *The Christian Healing Ministry*. SPCK 1981.
Kelsey, M. T., *Healing and Christianity*. SCM Press 1973.

Other books that may be found useful:

Glennon, J., *Your healing is within you*. Hodder & Stoughton 1984.
Glennon, J., *How can I find Healing?* Hodder & Stoughton 1981.
Wilkinson, J., *Health and Healing*. Handsel Press 1980. Notable for its detailed and careful exposition of biblical words and texts connected with healing.
Sanford, J. A., *Healing and Wholeness*. Paulist Press 1977. A fascinating and enlightening book which views the phenomenon of healing from a Jungian perspective. Unfortunately it was not known to me when writing my own book, but is to be highly recommended.

Index